Dusty's Cookies!

- 2 c margerine (or 1 c butter + 1 c marg.)
- 1½ c white suger
- 1½ c brown suger
- 2 eggs
- 2¼ c flour
- 2 tsp baking powder
- shake of salt
- 4½ c oats (quickcook oats)
- 1 c coconut
- 1½ c chocolate chips
- optional: 1 c rasins/crasins/berries
- 1 tsp vanilla

Bake: 350°C
         8-10 min (ovendependant)

500

chocolate delights

500

chocolate delights

the only chocolate compendium you'll ever need

Lauren Floodgate

SELLERS
PUBLISHING

A Quintet Book

Published by Sellers Publishing, Inc.
161 John Roberts Road, South Portland, Maine 04106

For ordering information:
(800) 625-3386 Toll Free
(207) 772-6814 Fax

Visit our Web site: www.rsvp.com • E-mail: rsp@rsvp.com

President and Publisher: Ronnie Sellers
Publishing Director: Robin Haywood
Managing Editor: Mary Baldwin
Senior Editor: Megan Hiller

ISBN: 978-1-56906-994-3
QUIN.FCCS

This book was designed and produced by
Quintet Publishing Limited
6 Blundell Street
London N7 9BH
United Kingdom

Library of Congress Control Number: 2007923859

Editor: Marianne Canty
Art Editor: Dean Martin
Designer: Jason Anscomb
Photographer: Simon Pask
Home Economists: Wendy Sweetser, Jacqueline Bellefontaine

10 9 8 7 6 5 4 3 2

Manufactured in Singapore by Pica Digital Pte Ltd.
Printed in China by SNP Leefung Printers Ltd.

contents

introduction

Some people like it as a hot drink, some like it in a luxurious cake, while others prefer it as an ice cold dessert. You can crave it, be addicted to it, and it's been found to cheer people up. So what is this superfood? Chocolate of course. However you like to eat it, there is no other food that people feel quite so passionately as they do about chocolate.

The range of chocolate produced today is phenomenal, with every possible combination of flavors and textures. The five main types of chocolate are white, milk, semisweet, bittersweet, and unsweetened; and every type is available in a variety of forms such as creamy, rich, flavored, or nutty. It can be delicately flavored or pack a punch with unexpected ingredients like chili. The chocolate delights in this book come in all shapes and sizes. Some recipes include chocolate or cocoa in the mixture, while others are topped, dipped, coated, or decorated in chocolate; but all these recipes have one thing in common, they all feature this universally adored ingredient.

Many classic chocolate recipes have been included from around the world. Some are served frosted or filled, while others, such as Sachertorte, are served coated with a shiny ultra-smooth chocolate sauce. Some cakes such as the black forest gateau feature stunning easy-to-make chocolate decorations made by painting fresh rose leaves. There are also no-bake bars that are bound together with melted chocolate, butter, and syrup and chilled in the refrigerator to set. If you crave something rich and deeply indulgent why not try the double chocolate mousse. You'll also find desserts that are perfect for serving to the family: chocolate cream tart with its fluffy chocolate layer and fudgy chocolate pudding that can be eaten hot or cold — perfect comfort foods for when only something chocolaty will do.

However you choose to eat yours, be it in a sauce, drink, ice cream, cake, muffin, cookie, petit four, or dessert, once you get started on the chocolate delights in this book you'll find yourself returning again and again to recipes that are sure to become firm favorites with all of your family and friends.

the history of chocolate

Chocolate can be traced back to the ancient Maya and Aztec civilizations of Central America, who made a spicy drink from cocoa beans. But it was not until Columbus's discovery of America in 1492 that news of "cocoa" reached the Old World. When Hernando Cortex conquered Mexico in 1519 the commercial possibilities of chocolate became apparent.

The Aztec Indians prepared a warm drink called "chocolatl," meaning warm liquid. This "food for the gods" was very bitter and the Spaniards didn't take to it at first; they made it more palatable by adding sugar and spices such as vanilla and cinnamon, and also serving it hot. This new and sophisticated drink was highly prized and the Spanish aristocracy began planting and growing cocoa in their newly acquired oversees colonies, where they kept the art of chocolate-making secret from the rest of the world for another hundred years.

Unfortunately the Spanish monks who processed the cocoa beans accidentally let the secret out and chocolate quickly became popular throughout Europe as a health-giving drink, with chocolate houses appearing in Great Britain around 1657.

With the advent of the steam engine the hand-production method was superseded and chocolate was mass-produced for the first time. By 1730 the price of chocolate had dropped dramatically, making it affordable to the masses, and in 1828 the cocoa press was invented which helped to improve the quality of the drink by removing part of the cocoa butter, the fat that naturally occurs in cocoa beans. This improved the flavor and gave chocolate its recognizable smoothness.

Chocolate was exclusively for drinking until 1847 when the British firm Fry and Sons introduced "eating chocolate," then in 1876 in Vevey, Switzerland, Daniel Peter devised a way to combine milk with chocolate to produce what we know today as milk chocolate. About this time in Holland cocoa powder was developed (hence the term Dutch-processed), which was less rich but more soluble than chocolate. This made it more easily digestible, nourishing, and therefore ideal for children.

making chocolate

Making chocolate is an art — even an ordinary bar of chocolate takes between two and four days to manufacture. Although the manufacturing process is specific to each company, there is a general processing pattern followed around the world.

cleaning & roasting
Processing starts with the cleaning of the beans to remove any debris, before the beans are weighed and blended according to the specific recipe of the brand. The beans are then roasted at 250°F (120°C) for 30 minutes to 2 hours during which they turn a rich dark brown and the characteristic flavor starts to develop.

shelling, crushing & pressing
The beans are then shelled to reveal the "meat" or "nibs," which contain about 53% cocoa butter. The nibs are then crushed to extract the cocoa butter which is known as chocolate liquor. The chocolate liquor is then put under intense pressure to remove the cocoa butter which drains away to be used later in the chocolate-making process. The pressed cake that is left after the removal of the cocoa butter is pulverized and sieved to make cocoa powder.

conching
While cocoa is made by removing some of the cocoa butter, eating chocolate is made by adding it. The mixture now undergoes "conching," a process of kneading to develop the flavor. At this stage other ingredients and flavorings can also be introduced.

tempering
The mixture is then tempered, a process of interval-heating, cooling, and reheating before being shaped in molds. Tempering stabilizes the cocoa butter crystals to make them more uniform in size. It also makes the chocolate snap when you break it.

types of chocolate

The main types of chocolate are white, milk, semisweet, bittersweet, unsweetened, and cocoa. These are generally produced with ordinary cacao beans (mass-produced and cheap) or specialty cacao beans (aromatic and expensive), or a mixture of the two. The composition of the mixture, origin of the cacao beans, and the roasting and the manufacturing process all affect the flavor and texture of the chocolate.

white chocolate: this is made with cocoa butter, sugar, milk, emulsifier, vanilla, and sometimes other flavorings, and has a mild creamy flavor. Because it doesn't contain any cocoa solids many purists don't consider it to be chocolate. Some European countries don't allow it to be called chocolate.

milk chocolate: this type of chocolate is the most popular choice for confectionery and contains at least 10% cocoa solids, sugar, and milk.

semisweet & bittersweet chocolate: dark chocolate must contain at least 35% cocoa solids. Generally semisweet chocolate contains 35–40% and bittersweet chocolate has 50% or more, although the exact cacao content will depend on the brand of chocolate. Semisweet and bittersweet chocolate are used in baking and eaten in the form of confectionary.

unsweetened chocolate: this strong, bitter form of dark chocolate has 100% cacao content. It is used in cooking and baking.

cocoa powder: this is made when chocolate liquor is pressed to remove the cocoa butter. This results in a fine, bitter-tasting powder that dissolves easily, called natural cocoa powder. Dutch-processed cocoa powder has been treated with an alkali to neutralize its acids. It has a more delicate flavor and is usually used in baking as it does not react with baking soda.

flavored chocolate

Candy manufacturers such as Seeds of Change and Green & Blacks produce a range of flavored chocolate candy bars. These are available in specialty stores selling quality foods and organic products, as well as on the Internet. If you are unable to obtain flavored chocolate you can make your own — the recipes here make 2 oz. of chocolate, for larger amounts simply multiply the ingredients for every 2 oz. you require. See specific recipe instructions to determine the type of chocolate to use as a base.

orange chocolate: melt 2 oz. of chocolate in a double boiler. Add a few drops of orange extract and the zest of 1 orange, stirring until combined. Use melted, or cool to set.

mint chocolate: melt 2 oz. of chocolate in a double boiler. Add a few drops of mint extract, stirring until combined. Use melted, or cool to set.

coffee chocolate: melt 2 oz. of chocolate in a double boiler. Add 1 tablespoon cooled prepared espresso or use 1 teaspoon of instant coffee which has been dissolved in 1 tablespoon hot water, stirring until combined. Use melted, or cool to set.

using dairy-free & gluten-free products

Dairy-free chocolate can be difficult to find as most semisweet and bittersweet chocolates contain dairy products. Look for brands of chocolate that are pareve (dairy-free) — the Internet is an excellent source of information. Substitutes for dairy milk include soy milk and rice milk. Nut milks such as almond and hazelnut can also be used in the recipes, although these have a distinctive flavor. Nondairy margarines are suitable for baking — unsalted corn margarine, for example, works well as a butter replacement.

Generally gluten-free flour (all-purpose or self-rising) can be substituted directly for wheat flour. Many gluten-free flours are available including rice, potato, buckwheat, and maize. When adding gluten-free flour to wet ingredients mix very gently to avoid knocking the carbon dioxide and oxygen from the mixture. Use gluten-free baking powder produced from rice flour and gluten-free cocoa powder that is additive-free. Gluten-free products are available from health food stores and specialty retailers on the Internet.

glossary of terms

baking blind: pastry shells are often prebaked "blind." To bake pastry blind prick the bottom crust with a fork before lining with a sheet of parchment paper. Fill the crust with pie weights or dried beans and bake as per recipe. When the pastry has hardened, the weights/beans and paper can be removed and the pastry baked to brown.

bombe: a frozen dessert set in a mold or bowl that is often made up of several layers.

buttercream: a cream made by creaming together butter and confectioners' sugar until it is light and fluffy. It can be spread, smoothed, or piped and is easy to flavor.

buttermilk: a nonfat or low-fat milk to which bacteria is added to thicken it and give it its tart flavor.

chantilly cream: a vanilla-flavored, sweetened whipped cream.

choux pastry: a sweet or savory pastry that is twice-cooked and can be spooned or piped into shapes.

corn syrup: a simple sugar (also known as liquid glucose) with a thick syrupy texture that thins when warmed.

couverture chocolate: contains a high percentage of cocoa butter (at least 32%) and has a high gloss and fine flavor. It is often used by pastry chefs and has to be tempered before use.

crème Anglaise: a rich sweet sauce traditionally flavored with custard.

crème patissiere: a term used to describe custard pie filling thickened with flour.

curdles: when a real egg custard is cooked at too high a temperature it will separate and look curdled. To rescue a curdled sauce remove it from the heat and beat until smooth before reheating gently.

fondant frosting or sugar paste: a firm white decorative paste that can be colored and shaped.

ganache: a thick creamy chocolate mixture that can be used to decorate and fill cakes. It is made from cream and chocolate and can be flavored in many ways.

glace frosting: a quick-to-make liquid frosting that is used to decorate cakes and cookies. It dries very quickly.

parchment paper: is siliconized on both sides to provide a nonstick surface. It is ideal for lining cake pans and cookie sheets as it does not require greasing.

pastry: when making pastry it is important to handle the dough as lightly as possible and to keep it as cool as possible. Take care when rolling out the pastry — flour both the board and the rolling pin to prevent stretching the pastry, this will cause it to shrink when baked.

phyllo dough: a type of pastry that comes in sheets not much thicker than a sheet of writing paper. It is very hard to make and is usually bought ready-made.

pie weights: these are commercially made ceramic or metal baking beans, or dried beans used for "baking blind." They are added to the lined pastry shell to weigh it down while it cooks.

praline: a mixture of caramel and nuts. Made with an equal weight of each, the sugar is cooked to make a caramel to which the nuts are added. When cold the praline can be crushed.

springform pan: a loose-based cake pan that opens out slightly when the spring hinge at the side is released.

sugar thermometer: a special thermometer that will withstand the very high temperature that boiling sugar reaches.

tranche pan: a long, shallow rectangular pan that can have straight or fluted sides and a loose base.

tempering: a technique used for chocolate with high cocoa butter content and involves the melting, cooling, and rewarming of the chocolate to break down the cocoa butter. This improves its appearance and produces a glossy streak-free chocolate that sets very hard.

equipment

Most of these chocolate delights are incredibly simple to make, and you'll only need a few basic pieces of equipment.

scales, measuring cups & spoons
Correct measuring equipment is essential for successful baking. If the proportions of ingredients are incorrect, you may find that cakes don't rise properly or frostings do not set.

mixing bowls & spoons
A variety of mixing bowls is essential in the baker's kitchen. You will need a large bowl in which to make pastry and batter. Medium bowls are useful when letting fruit fillings release their juices, and small bowls are necessary for melting butter and chocolate, separating eggs, and mixing small quantities.

sieves
You will need a large sieve for sifting dried ingredients such as flour, cocoa powder, and confectioners' sugar.

muffin pans, other pans & individual cups
Muffin pans can be used for cupcakes and muffins. You can line them with paper baking cups or simply grease them before filling them with batter. Madeleine pans can be used to create delicate shell-shaped treats. Ceramic baking cups or espresso cups can also be used for individual chocolate desserts.

timers
It is advisable to always use an accurate digital timer.

mixing bowls & electric mixers

Electric mixers can be great time-savers for beating batter, dough, or frostings, and can be quite inexpensive. They are also helpful when extended beating is required, as with meringue, and whipped cream.

rolling pins & boards

Useful for rolling out dough and pastry. Marble pastry boards offer the smoothest, coolest surface on which to roll out, but a large wooden board will also work nicely.

cookie cutters

You can cut out cookie dough by hand using a sharp knife, though it is much easier to use cookie cutters. Small, shaped cookie cutters are useful for cutting out fondant frosting decorations.

palette knives & metal spatulas

Spatulas are useful for transferring uncooked rolled cookies onto cookie sheets and moving hot cookies to a wire rack. Palette knives are useful for spreading and smoothing frosting on cakes.

wire racks

After baking, some chocolate delights should be transferred to a wire rack to cool.

frosting bags

Frosting bags with different style and size nozzles are useful for piping meringue and decorating items with frosting.

chocolate decorations

Chocolate is a fabulous ingredient to work with, and one that can be shaped, colored, and manipulated to create pretty shapes to use when decorating cakes and desserts.

chocolate shavings: use the coarse side of a grater to create chocolate shavings. Make sure the utensil is dry and work quickly so that the chocolate does not melt. Chocolate grates easily straight from the refrigerator.

making shapes: pour melted chocolate onto a sheet of parchment paper and use a palette knife to spread it out to 1/12-in. (2-mm.) thickness. Leave to cool until the chocolate becomes cloudy but has not set. Dip a cookie cutter in hot water and use to stamp out chocolate shapes. Allow the shapes to set on a separate sheet of parchment paper.

ribbons: chocolate ribbons can only be made from unsweetened chocolate as it contains no cocoa butter and is very flexible and easy to work with. Spread the melted chocolate onto a nonstick cookie sheet and leave to set. Working away from you, push a wallpaper scraper shallowly into the sheet of chocolate. Let the end curl over and hold this up gently with your other hand. Continue pushing the scraper down the sheet of chocolate to form a long, wide ribbon. Use immediately.

chocolate leaves: using a small brush, thickly brush chocolate onto the underside of washed and dried rose leaves taking care not to get any on the top of the leaves. Allow to set in the refrigerator before carefully peeling away the leaf and discarding.

chocolate curls: hold a block of room temperature white or unsweetened chocolate and run a vegetable peeler up and down one side to make curls. The cheaper the chocolate the better it tends to curl.

cocoa dusted shapes: melt the chocolate of your choice and spread it on a nonstick cookie sheet. Before it sets dust it lightly with confectioners' sugar, cocoa, or a mixture of both. When just set and using a sharp plain knife cut the required shape into the set chocolate. Leave to set completely before using.

chocolate run outs: draw your design onto a sheet of parchment paper. Spoon a little melted chocolate into a frosting bag fitted with a writing frosting nozzle and trace around the outlines. Fill the centers with extra chocolate so that it flows into all areas of the design. Allow to set before carefully peeling away the paper.

special gifts

Many of these chocolate delights make wonderful gifts, especially if they are placed in an attractive basket or box. Fresh-baked "welcome" muffins or cupcakes are great in a flat basket, a colorful container packed with cookies is a lovely way to say thank you, and homemade truffles in a sophisticated box is a delightful gift for a dinner party host.

Some items are best packed in a single layer, with a little tissue paper tucked around them to ensure they don't move around as you transport them. You may also wish to add some decorative embellishments such as a ribbon or cellophane. To wrap a chocolate Easter egg, cut out a large square of cellophane, place the egg in the center, then pull up the edges around the egg and tie with ribbon.

everyday cakes & desserts

This lovely selection of classic family favorites

is sure to have everybody coming back for more.

From "cut and come again" cakes to simple

desserts, making a delicious chocolate treat

for the family couldn't be simpler.

double chocolate baked alaska

see variations page 38

This 70s "retro" dessert is a classic favorite — easy to make and enjoyed by all.

1-pt. (600-ml.) carton chocolate ice cream
3 oz. semisweet chocolate, grated
1-pt. (600-ml.) carton cookies-and-cream
   ice cream

3 egg whites
3/4 cup superfine sugar
8-in. (20-cm.) round chocolate sponge cake
   (approx. 1-in./2.5-cm. thick)

Place the chocolate ice cream in a large bowl, beat with a wooden spoon until softened. Line a 2-pt. (1-l.) bowl with enough plastic wrap to overhang the edges. Spoon the softened ice cream into the plastic wrap-lined bowl and spread evenly across the base and up the sides. Tip the grated chocolate into the bowl. Tip the bowl from side to side to coat the ice cream evenly with the chocolate. Fill up the bowl with the cookies-and-cream ice cream and smooth the top with the back of a spoon. Cover with plastic wrap and freeze for 2 hours, or until set. Preheat the oven to 400°F (200°C). In a medium bowl whisk the egg whites with an electric mixer until stiff peaks form. Beat in the sugar a tablespoon at a time, beating well between each addition, until the meringue is smooth and glossy. Set aside. Place the chocolate sponge on a parchment paper-lined cookie sheet and invert the ice cream "dome" on top. Remove the plastic wrap. Using a knife, cut around the edge of the cake to leave a 1-in. (2.5-cm.) border around the ice cream. Spread the meringue over the ice cream and sponge, ensuring no ice cream is exposed. Bake in the oven for 10 minutes, or until the meringue is pale golden brown all over. Serve immediately.

Serves 8

chocolate cream tart

see variations page 39

Make this for your favorite chocoholics. It is a dessert for children and adults alike.

1 cup chocolate wafer cookie crumbs
1/4 cup unsalted butter, melted
1 tsbp. sugar or honey
1 tbsp. all-purpose flour
4 large egg yolks
2/3 cup granulated sugar
1/4 cup cornstarch
1/4 tsp. salt

3 cups whole milk
4 oz. semisweet chocolate, melted and cooled
3 oz. unsweetened chocolate, melted and cooled
2 tbsp. unsalted butter, softened
1 tsp. vanilla extract
1 cup whipping cream, chilled
2 tbsp. confectioners' sugar
1 tbsp. Dutch-process unsweetened cocoa

Preheat the oven to 350°F (175°C). Combine the first 4 ingredients until they are well blended. Press evenly into a 9-in. (23-cm.) tart pan until the crust covers the bottom and sides of the dish. Bake for 10 to 15 minutes. Using a fork, beat the egg yolks in a small bowl. Combine the sugar, cornstarch, and salt in a large saucepan. Slowly whisk in the milk over medium heat. Continue whisking until the mixture reaches a boil. Cook for 1 minute, still whisking. Quickly transfer half the milk mixture to the egg yolks. Whisk to combine, then return the egg yolk and milk mixture to the saucepan. Return to a boil and cook for 1 minute, continuously whisking. Remove from heat. Stir the melted chocolates, butter, and vanilla into the milk mixture. Cover with plastic wrap or parchment paper to prevent a skin from forming. Let cool to room temperature before refrigerating for 2 hours to set. Fill the baked piecrust with the chocolate filling. Chill for 6 hours. Using an electric mixer, beat the cream with the confectioners' sugar until stiff. Remove the pie from the refrigerator. Top the filling with the cream and dust with cocoa. Refrigerate any remaining pie after serving.

Serves 6–8

chocolate & banana trifle

see variations page 40

Everybody loves trifle and this recipe is great when you need a dessert and need it fast.

2 cups prepared custard
3 oz. semisweet chocolate, broken into pieces
1 small chocolate jelly roll, thinly sliced
11-oz. can mandarin segments in natural juice

2 bananas
1 1/4 cups whipping cream
grated chocolate, to decorate

Empty the pie filling into a medium bowl, and set aside. In a double boiler melt the chocolate pieces. Let the melted chocolate cool for 5 minutes, then stir into the pie filling.

Divide the jelly roll slices between 4 serving bowls. Drain the mandarin segments, retaining the juice. Drizzle 1 tablespoon of mandarin juice over the jelly roll in the base of each bowl. Divide the chocolate pie filling between the bowls.

Cut the bananas into 1/2-in.-thick (2-cm.) slices and distribute the slices between the 4 bowls. Divide the mandarin segments between the 4 bowls.

Beat the cream with an electric mixer until soft peaks form. Spoon 1/4 of the whipped cream over each trifle. Sprinkle the grated chocolate over each trifle. Refrigerate until ready to serve.

Serves 4

mississippi mud cake

see variations page 41

This is a dense, moist chocolate cake that can be eaten as a teatime cake or as an indulgent dessert when served with whipped cream or ice cream.

1 cup plus 2 tbsp. unsalted butter
6 oz. semisweet chocolate, broken into pieces
1 2/3 cups light brown sugar, packed
1 1/4 cups hot water
1 tbsp. instant coffee

1 3/4 cups all-purpose flour
1/2 cup self-rising flour
1/2 cup Dutch-process cocoa powder
2 eggs, beaten
confectioners' sugar, to dust

Preheat the oven to 325°F (160°C). Grease a 9-in. (23-cm.) square cake pan and line with parchment paper. Place the butter, chocolate, sugar, water, and coffee into a double boiler and heat until melted. Stir until the mixture is smooth, then cool for 15 minutes.

Transfer the cooled chocolate mixture to a bowl, sift in the flour and cocoa, and stir in the eggs. Using an electric mixer, beat until smooth. Pour the batter into the cake pan and bake for 1 to 1 1/4 hours.

Remove the pan from the oven and cool for 10 minutes. Transfer to a wire rack to cool completely. Dust with confectioners' sugar and slice to serve.

Store in an airtight container for up to 5 days.

Serves 9

chocolate berry roll

see variations page 42

This lighter-than-air sponge can be enjoyed without feeling guilty.

3 eggs
1/2 cup superfine sugar
3/4 cup all-purpose flour
1/4 cup Dutch-process cocoa powder
1 tbsp. hot water
1 1/2 cups whipping cream

1 tbsp. confectioners' sugar
few drops vanilla extract
1 cup mixed blueberries, raspberries,
    and pitted cherries
6 tbsp. chocolate spread (store-bought or
    use recipe on page 267)

Preheat the oven to 425°F (220°C). Grease a 13 x 9-in. (33 x 23-cm.) jelly roll pan and line
with parchment paper. Combine the eggs and sugar in a bowl and beat with an electric
mixer until pale and thick. Sift in the flour and cocoa and slowly add the hot water. Fold the
mixture with a large metal spoon using a figure 8 movement. Spoon the batter into the pan
and bake for 8 to 10 minutes until well risen. Turn the cake onto a sheet of parchment paper.
Trim the edges of the cake using a sharp knife, then carefully roll up the cake with the paper
on the inside. Transfer the roll to a wire rack to cool. Combine the cream, confectioners'
sugar, and vanilla in a bowl and beat with an electric mixer until soft peaks form. Divide the
whipped cream between 2 bowls. Roughly chop half of the fruit and stir into 1 of the bowls
of cream. Unroll the cake, remove the parchment paper, and spread
with chocolate spread (see recipe on page 266). Top with the fruit-filled cream, carefully roll
up and transfer to a serving plate. Spread the second bowl of cream over the jelly roll and
decorate with the remaining berries.

Serves 8

chocolate victoria sandwich

see variations page 43

This classic cake is enjoyed by everyone, and is ideal for cake sales as it can be sold whole or by the slice.

4 eggs
1 cup unsalted butter, softened
1 cup superfine sugar
1 3/4 cups self-rising flour, sifted
1/4 cup Dutch-process cocoa powder
1 tbsp. milk

1/2 cup unsalted butter, softened
1 1/2 cups confectioners' sugar
1/4 cup Dutch-process cocoa powder
1 tbsp. boiling water
grated chocolate, to decorate

Preheat the oven to 350°F (175°C). Grease two 8-in. (20-cm.) cake pans. Combine the first 6 ingredients in a large bowl and beat with an electric mixer for 2 to 3 minutes, until smooth and thick. Divide the batter between the pans and level with a spoon. Bake for 20 to 25 minutes until well risen and a wooden pick inserted into the center of each cake comes out clean. Remove the pans from the oven and cool for 5 minutes. Transfer to a wire rack to cool completely.

Combine the remaining ingredients in a bowl and beat with an electric mixer until smooth. Spread 1/2 of the frosting over the bottom half of the cake, then sandwich the 2 layers together. Spoon the remaining frosting into a frosting bag fitted with a large star nozzle and pipe 10 rosettes of frosting around the top edge. Decorate with grated chocolate and dust with confectioners' sugar before serving. Store unfrosted in an airtight container for up to 3 days.

Serves 10

no-bake spiked cake

see variations page 44

To cut this cake into beautifully thin slices, run an unserrated knife under hot water before slicing.

2 tbsp. orange or coffee liqueur (or use orange juice if preferred)
12 graham crackers, broken not crushed
1/3 cup unsalted butter
3 tbsp. honey
6 oz. semisweet chocolate, broken into pieces

1 cup whipping cream, lightly whipped
1 1/2 cups whole mixed nuts, roughly chopped
1/3 cup dried apricots, chopped
1/2 cup candied cherries, halved
1/2 cup candied peel, chopped
Dutch-process cocoa powder, to dust

Line an 8-in. (20-cm.) tart pan with a removable base with plastic wrap. In a medium bowl drizzle the liqueur or juice over the graham crackers.

In a double boiler melt the butter, honey, and chocolate and stir until smooth. Remove from the heat and let cool for 5 minutes. Fold in the whipped cream, nuts, apricots, cherries, peel, and graham cracker crumbs. Stir until combined evenly.

Spoon the mixture into the prepared pan and press down well. Chill in the refrigerator for 4 hours, or overnight. Carefully invert the slice onto a dinner plate. Peel off the plastic wrap and discard. Dust heavily with cocoa and serve.

Store in the pan, refrigerated, for up to 3 days.

Serves 10

chocolate silk pie

see variations page 45

A chocolate pie that is as smooth as silk — how can you go wrong?

1 store-bought pie shell
4 oz. unsweetened baking chocolate
1/4 cup unsalted butter
1 cup granulated sugar
3 tbsp. cornstarch

3 large eggs
1 1/2 tsp. vanilla extract
2 cups whipping cream
1 tbsp. confectioners' sugar
1 oz. semisweet chocolate, melted

Preheat the oven to 425 F (220 C). Prick the surface of the pie shell with a fork and prebake for 20 minutes or until the crust is golden. Transfer to a wire rack to cool.

Melt the chocolate and butter in a double boiler. Remove from heat. Combine the sugar and cornstarch, add to the chocolate mixture, and stir until smooth. Using an electric mixer, beat the eggs on medium until they become light yellow and thick. Stir the eggs into the chocolate mixture and return to medium heat. Cook for 5 minutes, stirring constantly, until the mixture thickens and becomes glossy. Whisk in the vanilla. Remove from heat and cool completely. Using an electric mixer, beat 1 cup of the cream until stiff. Incorporate the chocolate mixture into the whipped cream, folding gently. Spread the filling evenly over the baked crust. Cover with plastic wrap and chill for 4 hours. Use an electric mixer to beat the remaining 1 cup cream and the confectioners' sugar until stiff. Top the filling with the whipped cream. To garnish, drizzle melted chocolate in lines over the cream. Refrigerate any remaining pie for up to 3 days.

Serves 6–8

mocha cream éclairs

see variations page 46

Although some will tell you that choux pastry can be frozen, it really is at its best eaten on the day that it is baked.

1/4 cup unsalted butter
2/3 cup cold water
1/2 cup plus 2 tbsp. all-purpose flour, sifted
2 eggs, lightly beaten

3/4 cup confectioners' sugar, sifted
1 tbsp. prepared espresso, cooled
1 1/4 cups whipping cream
2 oz. semisweet chocolate

Preheat the oven to 425°F (220°C). Put the butter in a small saucepan, add the water, and bring to a boil. Remove from the heat, transfer to a bowl, and add the flour. Beat with a wooden spoon until it forms a ball of smooth paste. Let cool for 2 minutes. Slowly add the eggs to the paste, beating well after each addition, until the choux pastry is smooth and glossy. Spoon the pastry into a frosting bag fitted with a large plain nozzle. Pipe eight 4-in. (10-cm.) lengths, well spaced apart, onto a large cookie sheet lined with parchment paper. Bake for 12 minutes until well risen and golden brown. Remove from the oven. Poke the base of each éclair with the tip of a knife to let the steam escape. Transfer to a wire rack to cool. In a small bowl, combine the confectioners' sugar, coffee, and enough cold water to make a smooth frosting. Beat until smooth. Cut each éclair in half and dip the tops in frosting. Transfer to a wire rack for the frosting to set. Whisk the cream with an electric mixer until soft peaks form. Spoon the cream into a frosting bag and using a large star nozzle, pipe cream onto the base of each éclair. Cover each éclair base with a frosted top. Melt the

chocolate in a double boiler. Spoon the chocolate into a frosting bag fitted with a small plain nozzle and pipe zigzag lines across the tops of the éclairs. Transfer to a wire rack. Although choux pastry is best eaten on the day that it is made, these éclairs can be stored refrigerated for up to 2 days.

Makes 8

sticky apple & chocolate cake

see variations page 47

Apple and chocolate is a great flavor combination! This firm but sticky cake travels well and is easy to slice, making it ideal for picnics.

1 cup unsalted butter
1 cup superfine sugar
3 eggs
1/2 cup Dutch-process cocoa powder
1/4 cup water
1/2 tsp. baking soda

2 green apples, peeled and quartered
1 1/2 cups self-rising flour
1 heaped cup confectioners' sugar
1 tbsp. Dutch-process cocoa powder
1 tbsp. unsalted butter
1 tbsp. milk

Preheat the oven to 325°F (160°C). Grease a 9-in. (23-cm.) square cake pan.

Place the first 8 ingredients in a food processor and process until the mixture is smooth and evenly combined. Spoon the batter into the prepared pan and bake for 1 hour or until well risen. Remove the pan from the oven and cool for 5 minutes. Transfer to a wire rack to cool completely. Put the remaining 4 ingredients in a double boiler and heat until melted. Stir until smooth, adding a little extra milk if the mixture is a little too stiff. Spread the frosting over the cake. Once the frosting has set, the cake is ready to serve.

Store in an airtight container for up to 3 days.

Serves 9

variations

double chocolate baked alaska

see base recipe page 19

cherry & chocolate baked alaska
Prepare the basic recipe, replacing the cookies-and-cream ice cream with
an equal quantity of Cherry Garcia ice cream.

mocha chocolate baked alaska
Prepare the basic recipe, replacing the cookies-and-cream ice cream
with an equal quantity of coffee ice cream.

tropical chocolate sorbet alaska
Prepare the basic recipe, replacing the cookies-and-cream ice cream with
mango sorbet, the chocolate ice cream with raspberry sorbet, and the
semisweet chocolate with grated white chocolate.

light raspberry & strawberry alaska
Prepare the basic recipe, replacing the chocolate and cookies-and-cream ice
creams with 2 cups each of light strawberry and light raspberry ice creams.

fudge brownie alaska
Prepare the basic recipe, replacing the chocolate and cookies-and-cream
ice creams with 2 cups each of vanilla caramel fudge and chocolate fudge
brownie ice creams.

chocolate cream tart

see base recipe page 20

mocha cream tart
Prepare the basic recipe, adding 2 teaspoons instant coffee granules to the sugar and cornstarch mixture before adding the milk.

chocolate cream tart with shortcrust
Prepare the basic recipe, replacing the chocolate wafer crumb crust with a store-bought pie shell.

chocolate-hazelnut cream tart
Prepare the basic recipe, replacing the melted chocolates with 2/3 cup chocolate-hazelnut spread. Reduce the sugar to 1/3 cup.

white chocolate cream tart
Prepare the basic recipe, replacing the melted chocolates with 7 oz. good quality white chocolate, such as Lindt or Baker's. Reduce the sugar to 1/3 cup.

chocolate-mint cream tart
Prepare the basic recipe, omitting the vanilla extract and replacing it with 1/2 teaspoon peppermint extract. Garnish with chopped Andes Crème de Menthe Candies.

variations

chocolate & banana trifle

see base recipe page 22

tropical chocolate trifle
Prepare the basic recipe, replacing the mandarin segments with 2/3 cup chopped fresh mango.

pineapple & ginger chocolate trifle
Prepare the basic recipe, replacing the mandarin segments with an 8-oz. can drained, chopped pineapple and the jelly roll with 8 thin slices of ginger cake.

black forest & chocolate trifle
Prepare the basic recipe, replacing the mandarin segments with 1 cup red cherry pie filling and the bananas with 1 cup fresh raspberries.

red cherry trifle
Prepare the basic recipe, replacing the mandarin segments with 3/4 cup red cherry pie filling.

tutti fruity trifle
Prepare the basic recipe, replacing the mandarin segments with 3/4 cup drained, canned fruit cocktail.

mississippi mud cake

see base recipe page 25

mocha glazed mississippi mud cake
Put 2 1/2 oz. semisweet chocolate, 2 tablespoons unsalted butter, 1 teaspoon instant coffee granules, and 1 tablespoon water in a saucepan and heat until melted. Stir in 1 cup confectioners' sugar and 1 tablespoon cold water and stir until smooth. Spoon over the baked cake and leave to set for 1 to 2 hours. Decorate with walnut halves.

marshmallow mud cake
Prepare the basic recipe, stirring 1 3/4 cups miniature marshmallows into the cake mix.

double chocolate mississippi mud cake
Spread 4 tablespoons hazelnut and chocolate spread over the top of the cake and sprinkle with 1/2 cup chopped walnut pieces.

M&M chocolate candies mud cake
Prepare the basic recipe, stirring 1/2 cup M&M chocolate candies into the cake mix.

hazelnut mud cake
Prepare the basic recipe, stirring 3/4 cup toasted chopped hazelnuts into the cake mix.

variations

chocolate berry roll

see base recipe page 26

chocolate strawberry roll
Prepare the basic recipe, replacing the berries with 1 1/4 cups sliced strawberries.

chocolate raspberry roll
Prepare the basic recipe, replacing the berries with 1 cup raspberries and decorating the roll with chocolate leaves, mint leaves, and fresh raspberries.

tropical fruit roll
Prepare the basic recipe, replacing the berries with 1 cup mixed chopped fresh pineapple, and mango. Decorate the finished roll with 2 tablespoons toasted flaked coconut.

honeycomb chocolate roll
Prepare the basic recipe, omitting the chocolate spread and the berries. Crush 2 oz. of honeycomb, stir into half the cream and use to fill the roll. Decorate with grated chocolate.

white chocolate chip jelly roll
Prepare the basic recipe, omitting the chocolate spread and the berries. Grate 2 oz. white chocolate and fold into the cream for the filling. Use to fill the roll and decorate with white chocolate-dipped strawberries.

variations

chocolate victoria sandwich

see base recipe page 29

victoria sandwich with chantilly cream
Prepare the basic recipe, omitting the frosting. Put 2/3 cup whipping cream,
2 tablespoons confectioners' sugar, and 1 teaspoon vanilla extract in a bowl
and whip until soft peaks form. Use to sandwich the cakes together.

toffee chocolate victoria sandwich
Prepare the basic recipe. Spread 3 tablespoons dulce de leche (chocolate
toffee sauce) over one cake half and top with the buttercream. Omit the
grated chocolate and replace with pieces of chocolate-coated fudge.

raspberry & chocolate victoria sandwich
Prepare the basic recipe. Arrange 1/2 cup raspberries over the filling. Omit
the chocolate and replace with 10 fresh raspberries and mint leaves.

vanilla & chocolate victoria sandwich
Prepare the basic recipe, omitting the cocoa and replacing with an extra
1/4 cup self-rising flour and 1 teaspoon vanilla extract.

orange & chocolate victoria sandwich
Prepare the basic recipe, omitting the cocoa and milk and replacing with an
extra 1/4 cup self-rising flour, 1 teaspoon orange extract, and 1 tablespoon
grated orange zest.

variations

no-bake spiked cake

see base recipe page 30

no-bake spiked cake petit fours
Prepare the basic recipe, spooning the mixture into a 7-in. (18-cm.) square cake pan. When set, slice into fifty 1-in. (2.5-cm.) cubes and serve in petits fours cups.

ginger no-bake spiked cake
Prepare the basic recipe, replacing the graham crackers with gingersnaps, and the apricots with 1/2 cup chopped preserved ginger.

maraschino no-bake spiked cake
Prepare the basic recipe, replacing the candied cherries with 1 cup drained, chopped maraschino cherries.

milk chocolate shortbread cake
Prepare the basic recipe, omitting the graham crackers and semisweet chocolate and replacing with 3 oz. crumbled shortbread and 6 oz. milk chocolate.

granola no-bake cake
Prepare the basic recipe, using orange juice and omitting the apricots and peel and replacing with 1 cup granola.

chocolate silk pie

see base recipe page 32

mocha silk pie
Prepare the basic recipe, adding 2 teaspoons instant coffee granules to the melted chocolate mixture.

chocolate silk pie in chocolate wafer crumb crust
Prepare the basic recipe, replacing the pie shell with a store-bought chocolate pie shell.

white chocolate silk pie
Prepare the basic recipe, replacing the unsweetened chocolate with 4 oz. white bakers' chocolate. Reduce the sugar to 1/4 cup.

butterscotch silk pie
Prepare the basic recipe, replacing the unsweetened chocolate with 1 cup butterscotch chips. Reduce the sugar to 1/4 cup.

mocha cream éclairs

see base recipe page 34

mocha cream buns
Prepare the basic recipe, instead pipe the choux pastry in 8 large rounds.

mini mocha cream éclairs
Prepare the basic recipe, instead pipe the choux pastry onto the cookie sheet in 20 short lengths. Serve in petits fours cups.

mocha cream ring
Prepare the basic recipe, instead draw an 8-in. (20-cm.) diameter circle on parchment paper. Arrange spoonfuls of choux paste, slightly touching, around the circle. Bake for 20 minutes, or until golden brown. Drizzle with the frosting and melted chocolate.

praline & mocha cream buns
Prepare the basic recipe. While the frosting is still sticky, sprinkle each bun top with 1 teaspoon of finely crushed praline (use the recipe on page 168). Fold 3 tablespoons of praline into the whipped cream for the filling and omit the chocolate drizzle.

coffee ice cream éclairs
Prepare the basic recipe. Omit the cream and instead fill each éclair with a scoop of coffee ice cream. Drizzle with chocolate and serve immediately.

variations

sticky apple & chocolate cake

see base recipe page 37

pear & chocolate cake
Prepare the basic recipe, replacing the apples with 2 large, peeled
and cored pears.

banana & chocolate cake
Prepare the basic recipe, replacing the apples with 2 peeled
and sliced bananas.

apricot & chocolate cake
Prepare the basic recipe, replacing the apples with 4 ripe, halved
and pitted apricots.

peach & chocolate cake
Prepare the basic recipe, replacing the apples with 4 drained, canned
peach halves.

cookies

There's something very satisfying about baking a tray of cookies, especially when the kids want to join in and help, and these simple treats are at their best straight from the oven.

chocolate peanut butter kisses

see variations page 74

Loved by all and ideal for cake and cookie sales. The salty peanut butter gives these yummy cookies a distinctive nutty flavor.

1 cup light brown sugar, packed
1/2 cup unsalted butter
1 tsp. vanilla extract
1 egg, beaten
1/2 cup crunchy peanut butter

2 tbsp. milk
2 1/2 cups all-purpose flour
1 tsp. baking powder
1/2 cup semisweet chocolate chips

Preheat the oven to 375°F (190°C). Line 2 cookie sheets with parchment paper.

Combine the sugar, butter, vanilla, and egg in a large bowl, and beat until smooth. Beat in the peanut butter and milk. Sift in the flour and baking powder. Add the chocolate chips and stir until evenly mixed.

Scoop heaping teaspoon-sized portions of dough and roll into balls using well-floured hands. Evenly space the dough balls on the cookie sheets. Press flat with the back of a spoon and bake for 10 to 12 minutes, or until golden brown. Remove from the oven and cool on the cookie sheet for 5 minutes. Transfer to a wire rack to cool completely.

Store in an airtight container for 4 to 5 days.

Makes 24-30

chocolate chip shortbread

see variations page 75

The addition of chocolate gives a modern twist to a traditional Scottish shortbread recipe.

1 1/4 cups all-purpose flour, sifted
2 tbsp. cornstarch
1/4 cup superfine sugar

1/2 cup unsalted butter, diced
1/2 cup semisweet chocolate chips

Preheat the oven to 325°F (160°C). Line the base of an 8-in.-square (20-cm.) pan with parchment paper.

Sift the flour and cornstarch into a medium bowl, add the sugar, and stir to combine. Using your fingers, cut the butter into the mixture. Add the chocolate chips and knead well.

Turn the shortbread dough into the prepared pan and pack it down with the back of a spoon. Prick well with a fork and mark 8 wedges. Bake for 35 to 40 minutes until pale golden.

Remove from the oven and cool in the pan. Sprinkle with superfine sugar and serve.

Store in an airtight container for 4 to 5 days.

Serves 8

chocolate & raisin oatmeal cookies

see variations page 76

These cookies taste great warm from the oven and they'll disappear before your eyes!

3/4 cup all-purpose flour, sifted
1/3 cup self-rising flour, sifted
1/3 cup rolled oats
2 tsp. baking powder
1/3 cup light brown sugar, packed
1/4 cup superfine sugar

1 egg
1 tsp. vanilla extract
3 tbsp. sunflower oil
1/4 cup raisins
1/2 cup semisweet chocolate chips

Preheat the oven to 375°F (190°C). Line 2 cookie sheets with parchment paper.

In a medium bowl combine the flours, rolled oats, baking powder, and sugars. In a separate bowl beat together the egg and vanilla. Stir the egg mixture into the dry ingredients until just combined. Slowly add the oil to the mixture, beating well between each addition, until the mixture starts to come away from the sides of the bowl — you may not need to use all of the oil. Stir in the raisins and chocolate chips. Scoop heaping teaspoon-sized portions of dough and roll into balls. Evenly place the dough balls on the cookie sheets and flatten each cookie slightly with the back of a spoon. Bake for 10 to 12 minutes until pale golden.

Store in an airtight container for up to 3 days, or freeze for up to 3 months.

Makes 12-15

nutty coated double chocolate chip cookies

see variations page 77

These delicious cookies couldn't be easier to make.

1 cup all-purpose flour, sifted
1/3 cup self-rising flour, sifted
2 tsp. baking powder
1/3 cup light brown sugar, packed
1/3 cup superfine sugar
1 egg
2 drops vanilla extract

1/2 cup hazelnuts, halved
2 tbsp. semisweet chocolate chips
2 tbsp. milk chocolate chips
3 tbsp. sunflower oil
7 oz. orange-flavored semisweet chocolate
  (see page 10)
2 oz. white chocolate

Preheat the oven to 325°F (160°C). Put the first 10 ingredients in a food processor or bowl. Gradually add the oil, 1 tablespoon at a time, and process or stir until the mixture comes together to form a soft, crumbly dough. Scoop heaping teaspoon-sized portions of dough and roll into balls. Evenly space the dough balls on a parchment paper-lined cookie sheet. Bake for 10 to 12 minutes until golden. Remove from the oven and cool for 2 minutes. Transfer to a wire rack to cool completely. Place the orange-flavored chocolate in a double boiler and stir until melted. Dip the top of each cookie into the melted chocolate so that it is completely covered. Set on a wire rack for 10 minutes. In a double boiler melt the white chocolate. Using a fork, drizzle a little white chocolate over the chocolate top of each cookie. Allow the chocolate to set, then serve.

Store unfrosted cookies in an airtight container for up to 7 days.

Makes 12

ginger & chocolate chip cookies

see variations page 78

Chocolate and ginger combines beautifully. You can try sandwiching these cookies together in pairs using a good quality vanilla ice cream for a super quick dessert.

1 cup all-purpose flour, sifted
1/3 cup self-rising flour, sifted
2 tsp. baking powder
1/3 cup light brown sugar, packed
1/4 cup superfine sugar
1 egg

2 drops vanilla extract
3 tbsp. sunflower oil
3 oz. semisweet chocolate, roughly chopped
1/2 cup preserved ginger, minced
1/2 cup confectioners' sugar, sifted
2 tbsp. orange juice

Preheat the oven to 325°F (160°C). Put the first 7 ingredients in a food processor or bowl. Gradually add the oil, 1 tablespoon at a time, and process or stir until the mixture comes together to form a soft, crumbly dough. Stir in the chocolate and ginger and knead well. Scoop heaping teaspoon-sized portions of dough and roll into balls. Evenly space the dough balls on a parchment paper-lined cookie sheet. Bake for 10 to 12 minutes until golden.

Remove from the oven and cool for 2 minutes. Transfer to a wire rack to cool completely. Sift the confectioners' sugar into a small bowl and stir in enough orange juice to form a smooth paste. Using a fork, drizzle the frosting backward and forward across each cookie to make a crisscross pattern. Allow the frosting to set, then serve.

Store unfrosted in an airtight container for 5 days.

Makes 12

chocolate & lemon viennese fingers

see variations page 79

These elegant fingers are perfect served with mid-morning coffee.

for the cookies
1/2 cup unsalted butter, softened
1/4 cup confectioners' sugar
1 1/4 cups all-purpose flour
1/2 tsp. vanilla extract

for the frosting
4 oz. milk chocolate
1/3 cup unsalted butter
1 1/3 cups confectioners' sugar
2 tsp. grated lemon zest

Preheat the oven to 375°F (190°C). Line a cookie sheet with parchment paper.

In a medium bowl beat the butter and confectioners' sugar together until smooth. Stir the flour and vanilla into the creamed mixture. Spoon the mixture into a large frosting bag fitted with a medium star nozzle. Pipe sixteen 3-in. (7.5-cm.) fingers, well spaced apart on the cookie sheet. Bake for 10 minutes until pale golden brown. Remove from the oven and cool for 5 minutes. Transfer to a wire rack to cool completely. Melt the chocolate in a double boiler. Dip the ends of each cookie in the chocolate and transfer to a wire rack to set. Combine the butter, confectioners' sugar, and lemon zest, and beat until soft peaks form. Spoon the creamed mixture into the frosting bag. Pipe the frosting onto the base of half of the fingers, then sandwich together with the remaining fingers. Dust with confectioners' sugar and serve.

Store unfrosted in an airtight container for up to 2 days.

Makes 8

spiral cookies

see variations page 80

These are delicious served straight from the oven with vanilla ice cream.

for the vanilla dough
1/2 cup unsalted butter
1/2 cup superfine sugar
few drops vanilla extract
1/2 egg yolk, beaten
1 1/2 cups all-purpose flour, sifted

for the chocolate dough
1/2 cup unsalted butter
1/2 cup superfine sugar
1/2 egg yolk, beaten
1 1/4 cups plus 2 tbsp. all-purpose flour, sifted
1/4 cup Dutch-process cocoa powder

Preheat the oven to 350°F (180°C). Line a cookie sheet with parchment paper.

Beat the butter and sugar in a medium bowl until soft and creamy. Add the vanilla, egg, and flour into the creamed mixture and stir until it forms a soft dough. In a separate bowl, make the chocolate dough in the same way. Knead each dough separately until smooth, cover in plastic wrap, and chill for 30 minutes. Roll out both pieces of dough to 10 x 7.-in. (25 x 18-cm.) rectangles. Brush a little milk over the vanilla dough and lay the chocolate dough on top. Press down gently. Roll up from the short side to make a spiral log. Wrap and chill for 30 minutes. Cut the roll into 24 to 30 slices, arrange 1 1/2-in. (4-cm.) apart on 2 parchment paper-lined cookie sheets, and bake for 10 to 12 minutes until pale golden. Remove from the oven and cool for 5 minutes. Transfer to a wire rack to cool completely.

Store the uncooked dough, refrigerated, for up to 7 days.

Makes 24–30

white chocolate &
raspberry cookies

see variations page 81

Adding fresh fruit to cookies means they won't keep, so serve these warm from the oven with extra raspberries and a large scoop of vanilla ice cream.

1 cup all-purpose flour, sifted
1/3 cup self-rising flour, sifted
2 tsp. baking powder
1/3 cup light brown sugar
1/4 cup superfine sugar
1 egg

2 drops vanilla extract
3 tbsp. sunflower oil
1/2 cup white chocolate chips
1/2 cup fresh raspberries
1/2 cup confectioners' sugar, sifted
2 tbsp. rose water or orange juice

Preheat the oven to 325°F (160°C).

Put the first 7 ingredients in a food processor or bowl. Gradually add the oil, 1 tablespoon at a time, and process or stir until the mixture comes together to form a soft, crumbly dough. Stir in the chocolate and raspberries and knead well. Divide the dough into 12 portions and roll into balls. Arrange well spaced apart on a parchment paper-lined cookie sheet. Bake for 10 to 12 minutes until golden. Remove from the oven and cool for 2 minutes. Transfer to a wire rack to cool completely. Sift the confectioners' sugar into a small bowl and stir in enough rose water or orange juice to form a smooth paste. Using a fork, drizzle the frosting backward and forward across each cookie to make a criss-cross pattern. Allow the frosting to set, then serve. Store refrigerated for no more than a day.

Makes 12

chocolate puddle cookies

see variations page 82

Even when these cookies have cooled the fudgy center stays soft, giving these rich chocolate cookies a delicious chewy texture.

1/2 cup unsalted butter
3/4 cup superfine sugar
1 egg
1 1/2 cups self-rising flour
1/2 cup Dutch-process cocoa powder

1/2 tsp. vanilla extract
3 oz. milk chocolate
1 tbsp. melted unsalted butter
1 tbsp. light corn syrup

Preheat the oven to 350°F (175°C). Line 3 cookie sheets with parchment paper.

In a medium bowl beat the butter and sugar together until smooth. Beat in the egg. Sift the flour and cocoa over the mixture and then work in with a fork until a firm dough is formed. Scoop heaping teaspoon-sized portions of dough and roll into balls. Evenly space the dough balls on the cookie sheets. Bake for 15 minutes. Remove from the oven and make a dip in the top of each cookie with the back of a spoon.

Put the chocolate, butter, and syrup in a double boiler and heat until melted. Stir until smooth. Spoon a little of the melted chocolate into the dip in each cookie. Transfer to a wire rack to set.

Store in an airtight container for 4 to 5 days.

Makes 20

madeleine cookies

see variations page 83

You will need a traditional madeleine tray with seashell-shape indentations for these pretty treats.

1 1/4 cups self-rising flour
1/3 cup rice flour
1/2 cup cornstarch

1 cup unsalted butter
3/4 cup confectioners' sugar
4 oz. semisweet chocolate

Preheat the oven to 350°F (175°C). Grease an 18-mold madeleine pan.

Sift the flours and cornstarch together in a medium bowl. In a separate bowl beat the butter and sugar until smooth and creamy. Slowly add in the flour and work together to form a soft paste. Press a little of the mixture into each pan mold, smoothing the top of each with a spoon.

Bake for 15 to 20 minutes. Remove from the oven and cool in the pan. Gently ease the madeleines out, and transfer to a wire rack to cool.

Melt the chocolate in a double boiler. Dip the end of each madeleine in chocolate and allow to set. Dust with confectioners' sugar to serve.

Store in an airtight container for 3 days.

Makes 18

cream cheese & chocolate double deckers

see variations page 84

Crumbly cookies filled with a sweet cream cheese — simply luxurious.

1 cup all-purpose flour, sifted	3/4 cup superfine sugar
1/2 tsp. baking soda	1 egg
1 cup cream cheese	3 1/2 oz. bittersweet chocolate, melted
1/4 cup unsalted butter	1 cup confectioners' sugar, sifted

Preheat the oven to 350°F (175°C). Sift the flour and baking soda and set aside.

Beat half of the cream cheese and the butter until soft and smooth, then add the sugar and egg, and beat until light and fluffy. Stir in the chocolate and then the flour mixture. Mix to a smooth dough. Drop spoonfuls of dough onto baking sheets, and bake for 10 to 12 minutes until firm at the edges. Remove from the sheets onto wire racks, and allow to cool.

Beat the remaining cream cheese and confectioners' sugar until soft and smooth and spread on the bases of half the cookies. Sandwich with the remaining halves.

When completely cool, store in an airtight container in the fridge for 2 to 3 days.

Makes 24

chocolate whirls

see variations page 85

Pretty little cookies that taste as good as they look.

for the cookies
1 cup softened unsalted butter
1/2 cup confectioners' sugar
1 oz. bittersweet chocolate, melted
1 1/2 cups all-purpose flour
2 tbsp. Dutch process cocoa powder
3 tbsp. cornstarch

for the filling
1 cup softened unsalted butter
4 tbsp. unsalted butter
1 1/2 cups confectioners' sugar
1 oz. bittersweet chocolate, melted
2 tbsp. confectioners' sugar
1/2 cup confectioners' sugar

Preheat the oven to 350°F (175°C). Beat the butter and confectioners' sugar together until light and fluffy. Stir in the chocolate. Sift the flour, cocoa powder, and cornstarch and stir into the creamed mixture.

Pipe the mixture using a 3/4-in. (1.5-cm.) fluted nozzle into 2-in. (5-cm.) rosettes spaced 2 in. (5 cm.) apart on a nonstick cookie sheet. Bake for 10 to 12 minutes until golden. Allow to firm up slightly before transferring them to a wire rack to cool. Beat the butter and confectioners' sugar together until light and fluffy and stir in the chocolate. Spread the filling onto the bottom of half the cookies, and then sandwich together with the other halves. Dust with the 2 tablespoons of confectioners' sugar. Store the filled cookies in an airtight container for 3 to 4 days and unfilled cookies for 5 to 7 days.

Makes 18

chewy chocolate cookies

see variations page 86

Simply irresistible cookies, perfect for any time of day.

6 oz. bittersweet chocolate, chopped
1/4 cup unsalted butter
1/3 cup all-purpose flour
1/4 tsp. baking powder
Pinch of salt

2 eggs
1 1/4 cups superfine sugar
1 tsp. vanilla extract
4 oz. semisweet chocolate, chopped coarse

Preheat the oven to 350°F (175°C). Line 2 cookie sheets with parchment.

Melt the bittersweet chocolate and butter. Allow to cool slightly. Sift the flour, baking powder, and salt together. In another bowl, beat the eggs, sugar, and vanilla extract until thick and pale. Stir the melted chocolate into the eggs and sugar, followed by the flour and semisweet chocolate chunks.

Drop tablespoons of mixture onto the cookie sheets and bake for 8 to 10 minutes. Slide the parchment onto wire racks.

When completely cool, store in an airtight container for 2 to 3 days.

Makes 24

white chocolate chunk cookies

see variations page 87

For all those white chocolate fans — this one's for you.

1/2 cup (1 stick) unsalted butter
1 cup superfine sugar
1 egg
2 tsp. vanilla extract
1 1/4 cups all-purpose flour
1/2 tsp. baking soda

1/2 tsp. baking powder
1/4 tsp. salt
1/4 cup oatmeal
1 1/2 cups (8 oz.) chopped white
    chocolate chunks

Preheat the oven to 375°F (190°C). Beat the butter and sugar and then add the egg and vanilla. Sift together dry ingredients and stir in the oatmeal. Incorporate the mixed dry ingredients and chocolate into the butter mixture.

Roll into balls and use your fingers to flatten onto a nonstick cookie sheet 2 in. (5 cm.) apart. Bake for 8 to 10 minutes. Cool 5 minutes.

When cool, store in an airtight container for 4 to 5 days.

Makes 2 dozen

variations

chocolate peanut butter kisses

see base recipe page 49

chunky chocolate peanut butter kisses
Prepare the basic recipe, adding 1/2 cup coarsely chopped peanuts.

white chocolate peanut butter kisses
Prepare the basic recipe. Melt 6 oz. white chocolate. Dip the top of each cookie in chocolate and leave to set on a wire rack.

butter kiss ice cream sandwiches
Prepare the basic recipe. Sandwich the cookies together in pairs with scoops of your favorite ice cream and serve immediately.

party peanut butter kisses
Prepare the basic recipe. Sift 1 1/4 cups confectioners' sugar and stir in 2 to 3 tablespoons of orange juice to make a smooth frosting. Drizzle a little frosting over the top of each cookie and sprinkle with colored sugar.

butter kiss sandwiches
Prepare the basic recipe. Beat together 1 3/4 cups confectioners' sugar, 1/2 cup unsalted butter, and 1 teaspoon vanilla extract and use to sandwich the cookies in pairs.

variations

chocolate chip shortbread

see base recipe page 51

chocolate & cherry shortbread
Prepare the basic recipe, adding 3 tablespoons chopped candied cherries with the chocolate chips.

chocolate & ginger shortbread
Prepare the basic recipe, adding 1/4 cup chopped preserved ginger with the chocolate chips.

double chocolate shortbread
Prepare the basic recipe. Melt 3 oz. white chocolate and dip the outside edge of each wedge to coat thickly with chocolate. Allow to set on a rack.

chocolate orange shortbread
Prepare the basic recipe, adding 2 teaspoons finely grated orange zest and few drops of orange extract with the chocolate chips.

chocolate & almond shortbread
Prepare the basic recipe, omitting 1/4 cup all-purpose flour and replacing with 1/4 cup ground almonds and 1 teaspoon almond extract.

chocolate & raisin oatmeal cookies

see base recipe page 52

chocolate & cranberry oatmeal cookies
Prepare the basic recipe, replacing the raisins with 1/3 cup dried cranberries.

chocolate & brazil nut oatmeal cookies
Prepare the basic recipe, replacing the raisins with 1/3 cup chopped brazil nuts.

chocolate & cherry oatmeal cookies
Prepare the basic recipe, replacing the raisins with 3 tablespoons chopped candied cherries.

tropical chocolate oatmeal cookies
Prepare the basic recipe, replacing the raisins with 3 tablespoons dried, mixed chopped pineapple and mango pieces.

chocolate & macadamia oatmeal cookies
Prepare the basic recipe, replacing the raisins with 3 tablespoons chopped toasted macadamia nuts.

nutty coated double chocolate chip cookies

see base recipe page 55

macadamia coated double chocolate chip cookies
Prepare the basic recipe, replacing the hazelnuts with 1/2 cup roughly chopped macadamia nuts.

brazil nut coated double chocolate chip cookies
Prepare the basic recipe, replacing the hazelnuts with 1/3 cup chopped brazil nuts.

cherry & almond double chocolate chip cookies
Prepare the basic recipe, replacing the hazelnuts with 2/3 cup sliced almonds and the vanilla extract with almond extract. Replace the orange-flavored semisweet chocolate with 7 oz. milk chocolate.

raisin double chocolate chip cookies
Prepare the basic recipe, replacing the hazelnuts and semisweet chocolate with 1/2 cup raisins. Omit the orange-flavored semisweet chocolate and replace with 7 oz. milk chocolate.

coconut chocolate chip cookies
Prepare the basic recipe, replacing the hazelnuts with 2/3 cup dry flaked coconut and the orange-flavored semisweet chocolate with 7 oz. milk chocolate.

variations

ginger & chocolate chip cookies

see base recipe page 56

chocolate chip & coconut cookies
Prepare the basic recipe, replacing the preserved ginger with 1/3 cup dry flaked coconut.

cherry & chocolate chip cookies
Prepare the basic recipe, replacing the preserved ginger with 1/2 cup dried cherries.

apricot & pecan chocolate chip cookies
Prepare the basic recipe, replacing the preserved ginger with 3 tablespoons chopped dried apricots and 1/4 cup roughly chopped pecans.

gluten-free ginger & chocolate chip cookies
Prepare the basic recipe, omitting the all-purpose flour, self-rising flour, and baking powder, and replacing with the same quantity of equivalent gluten-free products (see page 10).

maple & chocolate chip cookies
Prepare the basic recipe, omitting the preserved ginger and vanilla and replacing with 1/2 cup chopped pecan nuts and 1 tablespoon maple syrup.

chocolate & lemon viennese fingers

see base recipe page 59

chocolate & orange viennese fingers
Beat together 1/2 cup softened unsalted butter, 1 3/4 cups confectioners' sugar, and 2 teaspoons finely grated orange zest until soft and fluffy. Use to sandwich the cookies together in pairs.

white chocolate & lemon viennese fingers
Prepare the basic recipe. Replace the milk chocolate with 5 oz. white chocolate.

dairy-free chocolate & lemon viennese fingers
Prepare the basic recipe, omitting the butter and milk chocolate and replacing with the same quantity of dairy-free equivalent (see page 10).

party viennese fingers
Prepare the basic recipe, omitting the milk chocolate and replacing with 4 oz. white chocolate. While the chocolate is still soft sprinkle each biscuit with colored sugar.

variations

spiral cookies

see base recipe page 60

stripy cookies
Prepare the basic recipe. Instead of rolling up the dough, cut the layered dough into four 7 x 2 1/2-in. (18 x 6.5-cm.) wide strips and pile the strips on top of each other to make a square log shape of alternate stripes.

abstract cookies
Prepare the basic recipe. Instead of rolling up the dough, pleat it backward and forward and shape into a square log using the flat of your hand, to make a log shape.

double chocolate chip spiral cookies
Prepare the basic recipe. Add 1/2 cup white chocolate chips to the vanilla dough and 1/2 cup semisweet chocolate chips to the chocolate dough.

gluten-free spiral cookies
Prepare the basic recipe, replacing the flour and cocoa powder with an equal quantity of equivalent gluten-free products (see page 10).

almond & chocolate spiral cookies
Prepare the basic recipe. In the vanilla dough replace 1/2 cup all-purpose flour and the vanilla extract with 1/2 cup ground almonds and almond extract.

variations

white chocolate & raspberry cookies

see base recipe page 63

white chocolate & pecan cookies
Prepare the basic recipe, replacing the raspberries with 1/2 cup coarsely
chopped pecan nuts.

white chocolate & blueberry cookies
Prepare the basic recipe, replacing the raspberries with 1/2 cup dried
blueberries.

white chocolate & sour cherry cookies
Prepare the basic recipe, replacing the raspberries with 1/2 cup dried sour
cherries.

white chocolate & cranberry cookies
Prepare the basic recipe, replacing the raspberries with 1/2 cup
dried cranberries.

white chocolate & macadamia cookies
Prepare the basic recipe, replacing the raspberries with 1/2 cup chopped
macadamias.

variations

chocolate puddle cookies

see base recipe page 64

white chocolate puddle cookies
Prepare the basic recipe, replacing the milk chocolate with 3 oz. white chocolate.

minty puddle cookies
Prepare the basic recipe, replacing the vanilla extract and milk chocolate with 1/2 teaspoon peppermint extract and 3 oz. mint-flavored semisweet chocolate (see page 10).

chocolate–orange puddle cookies
Prepare the basic recipe, replacing the vanilla with 1/2 teaspoon orange extract and stirring in 2 teaspoons grated orange zest. Replace the milk chocolate with 3 oz. orange-flavored semisweet chocolate (see page 10).

maple chocolate puddle cookies
Prepare the basic recipe, replacing the corn syrup with 1 tablespoon maple syrup. Press a toasted pecan into the soft chocolate on top of each cookie.

coffee puddle cookies
Prepare the basic recipe, replacing the vanilla extract and milk chocolate with 1 teaspoon prepared espresso, cooled, and 3 oz. coffee-flavored semisweet chocolate (see page 10).

madeleine cookies

see base recipe page 67

almond madeleine cookies
Prepare the basic recipe, replacing the rice flour with 1/2 cup
ground almonds.

orange madeleine cookies
Prepare the basic recipe, adding 2 teaspoons finely grated orange zest.
Replace the semisweet chocolate with 4 oz. orange-flavored semisweet
chocolate (see page 10).

coffee madeleine cookies
Prepare the basic recipe, stirring in 1 tablespoon prepared espresso, cooled.
Replace the semisweet chocolate with 4 oz. coffee-flavored semisweet
chocolate (see page 10).

lemon madeleine cookies
Prepare the basic recipe, adding 2 teaspoons finely grated lemon zest
and replacing the semisweet chocolate with 4 oz. white chocolate.

hazelnut madeleine cookies
Prepare the basic recipe, replacing the rice flour with 1/2 cup
ground hazelnuts.

variations

cream cheese & chocolate double deckers

see base recipe page 68

cream cheese, walnut & chocolate double deckers
Prepare the basic cookie dough and add 1/2 cup coarsely chopped walnuts to the batter.

cream cheese & white chocolate double deckers
Prepare the basic cookie dough and add 1/2 cup white chocolate chips to the batter.

cream cheese, raisin & chocolate double deckers
Prepare the basic cookie dough and add 1/2 cup raisins to the batter.

chocolate whirls

see base recipe page 71

dipped chocolate whirls
Prepare the basic cookie dough and then half-dip the filled cookies in melted bittersweet chocolate.

chocolate & ginger whirls
Prepare the basic cookie dough, adding 1 teaspoon ground ginger to the flour and 2 tablespoons chopped candied ginger to the filling.

chocolate cinnamon & raisin whirls
Prepare the basic cookie dough, adding 1 teaspoon ground cinnamon to the flour and 2 tablespoons raisins to the filling.

variations

chewy chocolate cookies

see base recipe page 72

chewy chocolate walnut cookies
Prepare the basic cookie dough and add 1/2 cup coarsely chopped walnuts.

chewy chocolate cherry cookies
Prepare the basic cookie dough and add 1/2 cup chopped natural candied cherries.

chewy chocolate & raisin cookies
Prepare the basic cookie dough and add 1/2 cup raisins.

amaretto-spiked chewy chocolate cookies
Prepare the basic cookie dough and add 1 tablespoon amaretto liqueur with the egg and vanilla.

chewy chocolate & espresso cookies
Prepare the basic cookie dough and add 1 tablespoon of cold, freshly made, strong espresso with the egg and vanilla.

white chocolate chunk cookies

see base recipe page 73

white chocolate chunk & raisin cookies
Prepare the basic cookie dough and add 1/2 cup raisins with the white chocolate chunks.

bittersweet-dipped white chocolate chunk cookies
Prepare the basic cookie dough. When the cookies are baked and cool, dip half of each cookie in melted bittersweet chocolate and place on parchment until the chocolate is set.

white chocolate chunk & pecan cookies
Prepare the basic cookie dough and add 1/2 cup chopped pecans with the white chocolate chunks.

white chocolate chunk & cranberry cookies
Prepare the basic cookie dough and add 1/2 cup dried cranberries with the white chocolate chunks.

dark-dipped apricot & white chocolate chunk cookies
Prepare the basic cookie dough adding 1/2 cup chopped dried apricots with the white chocolate chunks. When the cookies are baked and cool, dip half of each cookie in melted chocolate and place on parchment until the chocolate is set.

muffins & cupcakes

Whether you're making these as part of a decadent brunch, for a morning coffee, or to pile in a basket and give to a new neighbor as a welcome gift, muffins and cupcakes are easy to make and endlessly versatile.

cherry cupcakes

see variations page 116

Chocolate baskets filled with Kirsch cream and fresh cherries are delightful treats to serve at a dinner party.

8 oz. semisweet chocolate
1/2 cup unsalted butter
4 tbsp. light corn syrup
5 1/2 cups cornflakes
1 1/4 cups whipping cream

1 tbsp. confectioners' sugar
2 tbsp. Kirsch or brandy
2 cups fresh cherries, pitted
    and finely chopped
12 fresh cherries to decorate

Place the chocolate, butter, and syrup in a double boiler. Allow the chocolate to melt completely before stirring. Put the cornflakes in a plastic food bag and crush lightly with a rolling pin. Add the cornflakes to the melted chocolate and stir to coat evenly.

Divide the chocolate mixture between 12 cups of a nonstick muffin pan. Using a teaspoon, press the mixture into the base and up the side of each cup. Chill in the refrigerator.

Combine the cream and confectioners' sugar in a bowl and beat until smooth. Fold in the liqueur. Remove the muffin pan from the refrigerator. Using a palette knife carefully remove the chocolate cups from the pan. Divide the chopped cherries between the cups. Top each with a dollop or swirl of cream and top with a fresh cherry. Chill until required.

Serve decorated with fresh mint leaves, if desired.

Makes 12

coconut & chocolate cupcakes

see variations page 117

Toasted coconut and creamy white chocolate — a sensational combination that will keep you coming back for more!

4 eggs
2/3 cup superfine sugar
1 cup self-rising flour
1 tsp. baking powder

1 cup dry unsweetened flaked coconut
1/2 cup unsalted butter, melted
4 oz. white chocolate chunks
2 tbsp. toasted flaked coconut

Preheat the oven to 400°F (200°C). Line two 12-cup muffin pans with paper baking cups.

Combine the eggs and sugar in a large bowl and beat with an electric mixer for 2 to 3 minutes, until smooth. Sift the flour and baking powder over the top of the creamed mixture. Using a metal spoon, lightly fold in the flour using a figure of 8 movement. Add the coconut and melted butter and continue to fold in gently. Divide the mixture between the cups. Bake for 10 minutes, or until well risen and golden brown.

Remove from the oven and cool for 5 minutes. Transfer to a wire rack to cool completely.

Melt the chocolate in a double boiler, and stir until smooth. Using a fork, drizzle a little melted chocolate over the top of each cupcake and sprinkle with coconut. Allow the chocolate to cool completely before serving.

Store in an airtight container for up to 4 days.

Makes 24

vanilla cupcakes with chocolate frosting

see variations page 118

These fun cupcakes will brighten up any kid's party.

3 eggs
3/4 cup superfine sugar
1 1/2 cups self-rising flour
3/4 cups unsalted butter or margarine
1 tsp. vanilla extract

1 cup unsalted butter, softened
1 cup confectioners' sugar, sifted
3 tbsp. Dutch-process cocoa powder
1 tbsp. milk
M&Ms to decorate

Preheat the oven to 350°F (180°C). Line two 12-cup muffin pans with paper baking cups.

Put the first 5 ingredients in a large bowl and beat with an electric mixer for 3 to 4 minutes, until the mixture is smooth and pale. Divide the mixture between the cups. Bake for 15 minutes until well risen and golden brown. Remove from the oven and cool for 5 minutes. Transfer to a wire rack to cool completely.

Combine the butter, confectioners' sugar, cocoa, and milk in a large bowl and beat until smooth. Spoon into a frosting bag fitted with a medium star nozzle and pipe a large swirl of frosting on top of each cupcake. Scatter each cupcake with 5 or 6 M&Ms.

Store in an airtight container for up to 2 days.

Makes 24

cappuccino cupcakes

see variations page 119

This unusual frosting only takes a couple of minutes to make. Once these cupcakes are frosted you can let them set or eat while they're still sticky – it's up to you!

3 eggs
3/4 cup superfine sugar
1 1/4 cups self-rising flour
1/4 cup Dutch-process cocoa powder
3/4 cup unsalted butter or margarine
1/2 cup semisweet chocolate chips

1 tbsp. milk
4 oz. white chocolate chips
2 1/2 tbsp. cold black strong coffee
1 cup confectioners' sugar, sifted
3 tbsp. chocolate sprinkles

Preheat the oven to 350°F (180°C). Line 2 12-cup muffin pans with paper baking cups.

Combine the first 7 ingredients in a large bowl and beat for 3 to 4 minutes with an electric mixer until smooth. Divide the mixture between the cups and bake for 15 minutes until well risen and golden brown. Remove from the oven and cool for 5 minutes. Transfer to a wire rack to cool completely.

Put the white chocolate chips and coffee in a double boiler and heat until melted. Remove from the heat and stir in the confectioners' sugar. Spread the frosting over the cupcakes and sprinkle with the chocolate sprinkles. Store in an airtight container for up to 4 days.

Makes 24

white chocolate & raspberry cupcakes

see variations page 120

Sweet juicy raspberries and creamy white chocolate go together so well. These delicious light and fluffy cupcakes are perfect served with afternoon tea.

3 eggs
3/4 cup superfine sugar
1 1/2 cups self-rising flour
3/4 cup unsalted butter or margarine
2/3 cup fresh raspberries
2/3 cup white chocolate chips

1 1/4 cups whipping cream
2 tbsp. confectioners' sugar
1 tsp. vanilla extract
12 fresh raspberries, to decorate
fresh mint leaves, to decorate

Preheat the oven to 350°F (175°C). Line two 12-cup muffin pans with paper baking cups. Combine the eggs, sugar, flour, and butter in a large bowl. Beat for 3 to 4 minutes with an electric mixer until the mixture is pale and smooth. Gently fold in the raspberries and chocolate chips. Divide the mixture between the paper baking cups and bake for 15 minutes until well risen and golden brown. Remove from the oven and cool for 5 minutes. Transfer to a wire rack to cool completely.

Beat the cream, confectioners' sugar, and vanilla with an electric mixer until soft peaks form. Swirl the frosting over the cupcakes and decorate with a raspberry and mint leaves. Store unfrosted in an airtight container for up to 3 days. Use frosted cakes on the day they are decorated.

Makes 24

triple chocolate muffins

see variations page 121

Muffins are different than cupcakes in that muffins should be made quickly and the mixture stirred only until it comes together.

5 oz. semisweet chocolate
3 1/4 cups self-rising flour
1 tbsp. baking powder
1/2 cup Dutch-process cocoa powder
1/3 cup superfine sugar
2 eggs

2 tsp. vanilla extract
6 tbsp. sunflower oil
1 1/2 cups milk
5 oz. milk chocolate, roughly chopped
5 oz. white chocolate, roughly chopped

Preheat the oven to 400°F (200°C). Line 2 muffin pans with 20 paper baking cups.

Melt the semisweet chocolate in a double boiler. Sift together the flour, baking powder, and cocoa into a medium bowl and stir in the sugar. In a separate bowl beat the eggs, vanilla, oil, and milk. Stir in the melted chocolate. Stir the chocolate mixture into the flour and add the chopped chocolate. Do not beat — stir only until the mixture comes together.

Divide the mixture between the muffin cups and bake for 20 to 25 minutes until well risen. Remove from the oven and transfer to a wire rack. Dust with confectioners' sugar before serving. Serve warm or cold.

Store in an airtight container for up to 4 days. Suitable for freezing.

Makes 20

chocolate cheesecake muffins

see variations page 122

These are a combination of a cupcake and a cheesecake, with the texture of a muffin. These sophisticated marbled muffins are great with morning coffee.

1 3/4 cups self-rising flour, sifted
1 cup superfine sugar
1/2 cup Dutch-process cocoa powder
1 tbsp. baking powder
1 cup buttermilk
4 tbsp. vegetable oil

1/4 cup unsalted butter, melted
2 eggs
1 tsp. vanilla extract
1/2 cup semisweet chocolate chips
8 oz. package low-fat cream cheese, softened
1/3 cup sliced almonds

Preheat the oven to 375°F (190°C). Line a muffin pan with 16 paper baking cups.

Put the flour, 3/4 cup sugar, cocoa, and baking powder in a large bowl. In a separate bowl beat together the buttermilk, oil, butter, 1 egg, and 1/2 teaspoon vanilla. Add to the flour mixture and stir well. Stir in the chocolate chips, and divide the mixture between the cups.

Beat the cream cheese, remaining sugar, egg, and 1/2 teaspoon vanilla until smooth. Stir in the almonds and spoon over the chocolate mixture in the cups. Swirl together lightly. Bake for 20 to 25 minutes until well risen and a wooden pick inserted into the center comes out clean. Remove from the oven and transfer to a wire rack to cool. Store refrigerated in an airtight container for up to 4 days.

Makes 16

walnut–banana chocolate chip muffins

see variations page 123

This recipe is a great way to use sweet, overripe bananas.

1/4 cup unsalted butter
3/4 cup superfine sugar
1 egg
2 bananas, mashed
2 1/2 cups self-rising flour

2 tsp. baking powder
1 3/4 cups chopped walnuts
1/2 cup semisweet chocolate chips
1/2 cup buttermilk

Preheat the oven to 350°F (175°C). Line a muffin pan with 15 paper baking cups.

Beat the butter and sugar in a medium bowl until smooth. Beat in the egg and banana.

In a separate bowl combine the flour, baking powder, walnuts, and chocolate chips and stir well. Beat the nutty mixture into the creamed mixture, and stir in the buttermilk. Divide the batter between the cups and bake for 20 minutes until well risen and a wooden pick inserted into the center comes out clean. Remove from the oven and transfer to a wire rack to cool.

Store in an airtight container for up to 4 days.

Makes 15

orange & chocolate muffins

see variations page 124

This classic combination of flavors really is hard to beat. Using fresh-squeezed orange juice in the frosting will give it a delicate orange color.

11-oz. can mandarin segments, drained
2 cups self-rising flour
1 tsp. baking powder
1/2 tsp. ground cinnamon
1 tbsp. finely grated orange zest
1/2 cup superfine sugar
1/4 cup unsalted butter, melted

1 egg
5 tbsp. milk
1/2 cup semisweet chocolate chips
1/2 cup confectioners' sugar
3 tbsp. orange juice
grated chocolate, to decorate

Preheat the oven to 350°F (175°C). Line a muffin pan with 10 paper baking cups.

Roughly chop the mandarin segments and set aside. Combine the flour, baking powder, cinnamon, orange zest, and sugar in a medium bowl and stir well. In a separate bowl beat the butter, egg, and milk. Stir into the flour mixture until just combined. Stir in the chopped mandarin segments and chocolate chips and divide the batter between the muffin cups. Bake for 20 to 25 minutes until well risen and a wooden pick inserted into the center comes out clean. Remove from the oven and cool for 10 minutes.

Combine the confectioners' sugar with enough orange juice to form a smooth paste. Drizzle the frosting over the muffins and sprinkle each with grated chocolate. Transfer to a wire rack to set. Store in an airtight container for up to 4 days.

Makes 10

chocolate hazelnut cupcakes

see variations page 125

A timeless combination . . . with very little flour in the mix!

1/2 cup unsalted butter
1/2 cup semisweet chocolate chips
1/2 cup superfine sugar

4 eggs, separated
2 tbsp. all-purpose flour
1/2 cup chopped, roasted hazelnuts

Preheat the oven to 325°F (160°C). Place 12 paper baking cups in a muffin pan. Melt the butter and chocolate in a double boiler, or medium bowl over a pan of simmering water, stirring until completely melted. Cool slightly.

Beat the sugar and egg yolks in a medium bowl until thick and creamy. Stir the butter and chocolate, flour, and hazelnuts into the egg mixture.

In a medium bowl, beat the egg whites to soft peaks, and gently fold into the chocolate mixture. Spoon the batter into the cups. Bake for 20 minutes. Remove pan from the oven and cool for 5 minutes. Then remove the cupcakes and cool on a rack.

Store refrigerated in an airtight container for up to 2 days, or freeze for up to 3 months.

Makes 12

classic chocolate buttercream cupcakes

see variations page 126

The semisweet chocolate in this recipe gives the frosting a wonderful glossy sheen.

for the cupcakes
1 cup unsalted butter, softened
1 cup superfine sugar
1 1/2 cups self-rising flour
1 tsp. baking powder
4 tbsp. Dutch-process cocoa powder
4 eggs
1 tsp. vanilla extract

for the frosting
1 1/2 cups chopped semisweet chocolate
2 tbsp. whipping cream
1/2 cup unsalted butter, softened
1 1/2 cups confectioners' sugar, sifted

Preheat the oven to 350°F (175°C). Place 18 paper baking cups in muffin pans. Combine all the cupcake ingredients in a large bowl and beat with an electric mixer until smooth, about 2 to 3 minutes. Spoon the batter into the cups. Bake for 20 minutes. Remove pans from the oven and cool for 5 minutes. Then remove the cupcakes and cool on a rack. For the frosting, put the chocolate, cream, and butter in a pan over low heat. Stir gently until combined. Remove from the heat and stir in the confectioners' sugar until the mixture is smooth. Swirl onto the cupcakes.

Store unfrosted in an airtight container for up to 2 days.

Makes 18

mini peanut butter cupcakes

see variations page 127

Simple and no fuss. You can make these cupcakes in large batches, which makes them ideal for kids' parties and picnics.

2 oz. milk chocolate, broken into pieces
2 tbsp. unsalted butter

3 tbsp. whipping cream
1 cup smooth peanut butter

Place 12 mini foil baking cups in a muffin pan.

Place the chocolate, butter, and cream in a double boiler and stir until smooth. Remove from the heat and set aside.

With damp hands, shape the peanut butter into 12 small flat circles. Push the peanut butter into the bottom of the cups.

Pour the melted chocolate over the peanut butter, and refrigerate for at least 2 hours.

Store in an airtight container for up to 3 days.

Makes 12

chocolate ice cream cupcakes

see variations page 128

It's best to move these cupcakes from freezer to refrigerator 30 minutes before serving.

for the cupcakes
1 cup unsalted butter, softened
1 cup superfine sugar
1 1/2 cups self-rising flour
4 tbsp. Dutch-process cocoa powder
1 tsp. baking powder
4 eggs
1 tsp. vanilla extract

for the filling and glaze
1 cup chocolate ice cream
1/2 cup semisweet chocolate chips
1/3 cup whipping cream

Preheat the oven to 350°F (175°C). Place 18 paper baking cups in muffin pans. Combine all the cupcake ingredients in a medium bowl and beat with an electric mixer until smooth and creamy, about 2 to 3 minutes.

Spoon the batter into the cups. Bake for 20 minutes. Remove pans from the oven and cool for 5 minutes. Then remove the cupcakes and cool on a rack. When cool, slice the cupcakes horizontally and spread a little softened ice cream on the bottom slice. Place the top back on the cupcake and freeze. Prepare the glaze by melting the chocolate in a double boiler, or a medium bowl over a pan of simmering water, stirring until completely melted. Remove from the heat. Add the cream and stir until well combined. Cool slightly and spoon over the cupcakes. Return to the freezer to set. Freeze in an airtight container for up to 3 months.

Makes 12

chocolate mud cupcakes

see variations page 129

These cupcakes are so simple to make you won't hesitate to make another batch!

1 cup semisweet chocolate chips
1 1/3 cups unsalted butter
5 eggs

2/3 cup superfine sugar
3/4 cup self-rising flour
2 tbsp. Dutch-process cocoa powder, for dusting

Preheat the oven to 325°F (160°C). Place 12 paper baking cups in a muffin pan.

In a double boiler, or a medium bowl set over a pan of gently simmering water, melt the chocolate and butter together, stirring well. Leave to cool a little.

Beat the eggs and sugar in a large bowl until pale and thick. Fold the flour into the egg mixture and then stir in the melted chocolate and butter until well blended.

Spoon the mixture into the cups and bake for 20 minutes. The cupcakes will be soft and gooey in texture and appearance. Remove pan from the oven and cool for 5 minutes. Then remove the cupcakes from pan. Serve swiftly, dusted with cocoa powder.

Store in the refrigerator in an airtight container for up to 3 days.

Makes 12

cherry cupcakes

see base recipe page 89

raspberry cupcakes
Prepare the basic recipe, replacing the cherries with 1 1/3 cups
fresh raspberries.

strawberry cupcakes
Prepare the basic recipe, replacing the cherries 1 1/4 cups quartered
fresh strawberries.

kiwi cupcakes
Prepare the basic recipe, replacing the cherries with 3 peeled and
chopped kiwi fruit.

rum & raisin cupcakes
Prepare the basic recipe, replacing the cherries and Kirsch with
1/2 cup large raisins soaked in 4 tablespoons dark rum.

white passion fruit cupcakes
Prepare the basic recipe, omitting the semisweet chocolate, cherries,
and Kirsch and replacing with 8 oz. white chocolate and 4 seeded
passion fruit, folding the pulp into the whipped cream.

coconut & chocolate cupcakes

see base recipe page 91

raspberry, coconut & chocolate cupcakes

Prepare the basic recipe. Half fill each of the paper baking cups with
batter, put one fresh raspberry in the center of each, and top with the
remaining batter.

frosted milk chocolate cupcakes

Prepare the basic recipe. Half fill each paper baking cup with batter,
pop a chunk of chocolate in the center of each, and top with batter. Beat
1/2 cup unsalted butter, 1 3/4 cups sifted confectioners' sugar, and 1/2
teaspoon vanilla extract. Swirl the frosting on top of each cupcake and
sprinkle with coconut.

almond & chocolate cupcakes

Prepare the basic recipe, replacing the coconut with 3/4 cup ground almonds
and 1/2 teaspoon almond extract.

easter cupcakes

Prepare the basic recipe, omitting the chocolate chunks and coconut.
Beat 1/2 cup unsalted butter, 1 3/4 cups sifted confectioners' sugar, and
2 tablespoons cocoa powder. Pipe the frosting in a swirl on top of each
cake and decorate with chocolate eggs.

vanilla cupcakes with chocolate frosting

see base recipe page 92

choc chip vanilla cupcakes with chocolate frosting
Prepare the basic recipe, stirring 1/3 cup milk chocolate chips into the batter.

vanilla cupcakes with chocolate toffee frosting
Prepare the basic recipe. Replace the M&Ms with soft fudge pieces and drizzle 1 teaspoon store-bought toffee sauce over the top of each decorated cupcake.

mocha cupcakes with chocolate frosting
Prepare the basic recipe, replacing the vanilla extract with 1 tablespoon prepared espresso, cooled. Replace the M&Ms with grated chocolate.

marmalade cupcakes with chocolate frosting
Prepare the basic recipe, omitting the vanilla extract and stirring in 3 tablespoons orange marmalade. Stir 2 teaspoons finely grated orange zest and 1 teaspoon orange extract into the frosting.

halloween cupcakes
Prepare the basic recipe, adding a few drops of orange food color to the batter and the frosting. Roll out 2 oz. orange fondant frosting thinly, and stamp out Halloween shapes and use to decorate the cupcake tops.

cappuccino cupcakes

see base recipe page 95

black coffee cupcakes
Prepare the basic recipe replacing the white chocolate with 4 oz.
semisweet chocolate.

latte coffee cupcakes
Prepare the basic recipe replacing the white chocolate with 4 oz.
milk chocolate.

gluten-free cappuccino cupcakes
Prepare the basic recipe omitting the self-rising flour and cocoa and
replacing with the same weight of gluten-free self-rising flour and cocoa
(see page 10).

raisin & macadamia cupcakes
Prepare the basic recipe omitting the semisweet chocolate chips and
replacing with 1/3 cup each raisins and chopped macadamias.

almond & cappuccino cupcakes
Prepare the basic recipe omitting the semisweet chocolate chips and
replacing with 3/4 cup chopped toasted almonds.

white chocolate & raspberry cupcakes

see base recipe page 96

white chocolate & blackberry cupcakes
Prepare the basic recipe, replacing the raspberries with 2/3 cup
fresh blackberries. Use blackberries to decorate.

white chocolate & cherry cupcakes
Prepare the basic recipe, replacing the raspberries with 1 cup dried cherries.

white chocolate & blueberry cupcakes
Prepare the basic recipe, replacing the raspberries with 1 cup sweetened
dried blueberries.

black forest fruit cupcakes
Prepare the basic recipe, replacing the raspberries with 1 cup fresh
pitted cherries.

white chocolate & banana cupcakes
Prepare the basic recipe, replacing 2/3 cup raspberries with 2/3 cup
mashed banana.

triple chocolate muffins

see base recipe page 99

triple chocolate & orange muffins
Prepare the basic recipe, stirring in 1 tablespoon finely grated orange zest and 1 teaspoon orange extract with the wet ingredients.

triple chocolate & hazelnut muffins
Prepare the basic recipe, omitting 2 oz. white chocolate and replacing with 1/2 cup chopped roasted hazelnuts.

triple chocolate & pecan muffins
Prepare the basic recipe, omitting 2 oz. white chocolate and replacing with 1/2 cup chopped pecans.

gluten-free triple chocolate and orange muffins
Prepare the basic recipe, omitting the self-rising flour, baking powder, and cocoa, replacing with the same weight of equivalent gluten-free products (see page 10).

triple chocolate muffins with kahlua frosting
Prepare the basic recipe. Beat together 1 3/4 cups confectioners' sugar, 1/2 cup softened butter, 1 tablespoon grated orange zest, and 2 tablespoons Kahlua. Swirl Kahlua frosting onto the cooled muffins.

variations

chocolate cheesecake muffins

see base recipe page 100

chocolate–orange cheesecake muffins
Prepare the basic recipe, replacing the vanilla extract with 1 teaspoon orange extract. Stir in 1 tablespoon finely grated orange zest.

chocolate–lemon cheesecake muffins
Prepare the basic recipe, replacing the vanilla extract with 1 teaspoon lemon extract. Stir in 1 tablespoon finely grated lemon zest.

chocolate–lime cheesecake muffins
Prepare the basic recipe, replacing the vanilla extract with the grated zest and juice of 1 lime.

chocolate-banana cheesecake muffins
Prepare the basic recipe, replacing the sliced almonds with 1/2 cup sweetened banana chips broken into small pieces.

chocolate–hazelnut cheesecake muffins
Prepare the basic recipe. Spread the top of each muffin with 2 teaspoons hazelnut and chocolate spread and scatter each with 1 teaspoon toasted chopped hazelnuts.

walnut–banana chocolate chip muffins

see base recipe page 103

pecan–banana chocolate chip muffins
Prepare the basic recipe, replacing the walnuts with 1 3/4 cups
chopped pecans.

peanut–banana chocolate chip muffins
Prepare the basic recipe, replacing the walnuts with 1 3/4 cups chopped,
blanched peanuts.

macadamia–banana chocolate chip muffins
Prepare the basic recipe, replacing the walnuts with 1 3/4 cups
chopped macadamias.

brazil–banana chocolate chip muffins
Prepare the basic recipe, replacing the walnuts with 1 3/4 cups chopped
Brazil nuts.

cashew–banana chocolate chip muffins
Prepare the basic recipe, replacing the walnuts with 1 3/4 cups chopped,
unsalted cashew nuts.

variations

orange & chocolate muffins

see base recipe page 104

peach & chocolate muffins
Prepare the basic recipe, replacing the oranges with 1 1/4 cups finely chopped peach slices.

apricot & chocolate muffins
Prepare the basic recipe, replacing the oranges with 1 1/4 cups finely chopped apricot halves.

raspberry & chocolate muffins
Prepare the basic recipe, replacing the oranges with 1 1/4 cups chopped fresh raspberries.

passion fruit & orange chocolate muffins
Prepare the basic recipe. Omit 1 tablespoon of the orange juice and stir 2 tablespoons of passion fruit seeds into the frosting. Omit the grated chocolate.

lime & chocolate muffins
Prepare the basic recipe, replacing the orange juice with an equal quantity of lime juice. Omit the grated chocolate and decorate with fresh lime zest.

variations

chocolate hazelnut cupcakes

see base recipe page 106

chocolate hazelnut & cranberry cupcakes
Prepare the basic cupcake recipe, adding 3 tablespoons chopped dried cranberries to the egg mixture.

chocolate hazelnut & orange cupcakes
Prepare the basic cupcake recipe, adding 2 tablespoons finely grated orange zest to the egg mixture.

chocolate macadamia nut cupcakes
Prepare the basic cupcake recipe, substituting 1/2 cup roasted and chopped macadamia nuts for the hazelnuts.

variations

classic chocolate buttercream cupcakes

see base recipe page 108

white & semisweet chocolate buttercream cupcakes
Prepare the basic cupcake recipe, stirring 3 tablespoons mixed semisweet chocolate chips and white chocolate chips into the creamed batter.

macadamia nut-frosted buttercream cupcakes
Prepare the basic cupcake recipe. Lightly toast 1/2 cup macadamia nuts and chop finely. Stir the macadamia nuts into the frosting mixture after adding the sugar.

orange & semisweet chocolate buttercream cupcakes
Prepare the basic cupcake recipe, substituting 1 tablespoon orange zest for the vanilla extract.

mini peanut butter cupcakes

see base recipe page 110

mini marshmallow & peanut butter cupcakes
Prepare the basic cupcake recipe. Add 1 cup chopped large marshmallows to the melted chocolate mixture.

mini coconut & peanut butter cupcakes
Prepare the basic cupcake recipe. Add 3 tablespoons sweetened coconut to the melted chocolate.

mini jam & peanut butter cupcakes
Prepare the basic cupcake recipe. Place a teaspoon of your favorite fruit jam into the bottom of the baking cups and top with the peanut butter and then the chocolate.

variations

chocolate ice cream cupcakes

see base recipe page 112

vanilla ice cream cupcakes
Prepare the basic cupcake recipe, substituting 1 cup vanilla ice cream for the chocolate ice cream.

chocolate chip & mint ice cream cupcakes
Prepare the basic cupcake recipe, substituting 1 cup mint chocolate chip ice cream for the chocolate ice cream.

caramel ice cream cupcakes
Prepare the basic cupcake recipe, substituting 1 cup caramel swirl ice cream for the chocolate ice cream.

variations

chocolate mud cupcakes

see base recipe page 114

raspberry mud cupcakes
Prepare the basic cupcake recipe. Stir in 1/2 cup lightly crushed raspberries
to the mixture after adding the melted chocolate.

white chocolate mud cupcakes
Prepare the basic cupcake recipe. Substitute 1 1/2 cups white chocolate
chips for the semisweet chocolate chips.

macadamia mud cupcakes
Prepare the basic cupcake recipe. Toast and chop 1/2 cup macadamia nuts,
and stir them in after adding the melted chocolate.

bars

These homemade sheetcakes and cookie bars can be simple or glamorous enough to serve with after-dinner coffee. And since they keep and travel well, they are also great for picnics and lunch bags, or for taking to the office.

pecan brownies with sour cream frosting

see variations page 150

These deliciously rich and sticky brownies are ideal for a picnic or day out.

8 oz. semisweet chocolate
2/3 cup unsalted butter
2 eggs
2/3 cup superfine sugar
few drops vanilla extract

1/2 cup self-rising flour, sifted
1 cup pecans, chopped
4 oz. white chocolate, roughly chopped
1/4 cup sour cream

Preheat the oven to 375°F (190°C). Grease an 8-in. (20-cm.) square cake pan. Melt 4 oz. semisweet chocolate and butter in a double boiler, then remove from the heat.

Beat the eggs, sugar, and vanilla in a bowl. Stir in the melted chocolate mixture. Add the flour, pecans, and white chocolate and stir to combine. Pour into the prepared pan and bake for 30 minutes until the center is just firm to the touch. Set the pan on a wire rack to cool.

Melt the remaining semisweet chocolate in a double boiler. Remove from the heat and add the sour cream. Stir until smooth and glossy. Spread the frosting over the top of the brownie and chill until set. Cut into 9 squares to serve.

Store refrigerated in an airtight container for up to 4 days.

Makes 9

millionaires' shortbread

see variations page 151

This is seriously good and is wonderfully sweet too! This recipe makes a large quantity but it can be easily halved for a more modest amount.

2 1/2 cups all-purpose flour, sifted
1/4 cup cornstarch
2 cups unsalted butter, diced
1/2 cup superfine sugar

1 cup light brown sugar
two 14-oz. cans of sweetened condensed milk
8 oz. milk or semisweet chocolate

Preheat the oven to 325°F (160°C). Put the flour, cornstarch, 1 cup butter, and sugar in a food processor and process until the mixture resembles coarse meal. Turn into a 13 x 9-in. (33 x 23-cm.) jelly roll pan and pack down with the back of a spoon. Prick well with a fork and bake for 35 to 40 minutes until pale golden. Set the pan on a wire rack to cool.

Place the remaining butter and brown sugar in a saucepan over a low heat until melted. Add the condensed milk and bring slowly to a boil. Stir continuously until the mixture turns a pale caramel color, approximately 3 to 4 minutes. Pour over the top of the shortbread and level with the back of a wooden spoon. Chill in the refrigerator for 1 hour, or until set. Melt the chocolate in double boiler and spread over the caramel. Chill in the refrigerator until set.

To serve, cut into 15 to 18 slices using a sharp, unserrated knife.

Makes 15-18

chocolate & ginger granola bars

see variations page 152

Granola bars should be a pantry staple. They are wholesome and filling, and they make the perfect snack for that gap between breakfast and lunch.

1 1/4 cups unsalted butter
1/2 cup light brown sugar, packed
2/3 cup light corn syrup
5 1/3 cups rolled oats

1/2 tsp. ground ginger
1/3 cup milk chocolate chips
1/2 cup preserved ginger, chopped

Preheat the oven to 400°F (200°C).

Grease a 13 x 9-in. (33 x 23-cm.) pan and line the base with parchment paper.

Place the butter, sugar, and syrup in a saucepan and heat gently until melted. Stir in the remaining ingredients and spoon into the prepared pan. Press down with the back of a wooden spoon and bake for 15 minutes until pale golden.

Set the pan on a wire rack to cool for 5 minutes. To serve, cut into 15 slices.

Store in an airtight container for up to 3 days. This recipe is not suitable for freezing.

Makes 15

bittersweet chocolate crunchies

see variations page 153

These are everyone's favorite refrigerator cookie — and especially easy to make with kids.

7 oz. bittersweet chocolate
1/4 cup unsalted butter
5 tbsp. corn syrup
3 cups crisped rice cereal

Line 2 cookie sheets with parchment.

Melt the chocolate and butter together in a heatproof bowl over a saucepan of simmering water, or in the microwave.

Stir in the corn syrup and crisped rice cereal. Drop spoonfuls of the mixture onto the cookie sheets and refrigerate for about 45 minutes, until set.

Store in an airtight container in the fridge for 5 to 7 days.

Makes 2 dozen

chocolate–orange no-bake fruit bars

see variations page 154

This recipe also makes great petits fours when sliced into delicate cubes and served in pretty paper cups.

12-oz. package shortbread cookies
1/3 cup dried apricots
1/4 cup shelled pistachio nuts
1/4 cup sliced almonds, toasted
3 tbsp. candied cherries
1/4 cup preserved ginger

1/2 cup orange juice
1 tsp. vanilla extract
7 oz. white chocolate
3/4 cup unsalted butter
2 oz. semisweet chocolate

Line an 8-in. (20-cm.) round layer cake pan with plastic wrap. Break the shortbread cookies into small, bitesize pieces and place in a large bowl. Roughly chop the apricots and pistachio nuts and stir in with the cookie pieces. Add the sliced almonds and mix to combine. Chop the candied cherries and ginger and add to the bowl, followed by the orange juice and vanilla. Place 5 1/2 oz. white chocolate into a double boiler and add the butter. Heat until melted. Add to the cookie mixture and stir until evenly combined. Spoon the cookie mixture into the prepared pan and chill in the refrigerator for 4 hours. Melt the semisweet chocolate in a double boiler and drizzle over the top of the chilled slice. Repeat with the remaining white chocolate and chill in the refrigerator until set. To serve, ease out of the pan, discard the plastic wrap, and cut into 12. Store refrigerated in an airtight container for up to 3 days. This recipe is not suitable for freezing.

Makes 12

devil's food cake bars

see variations page 155

These delicious squishy slices will be demolished by the kids in no time.

2/3 cup margarine or unsalted butter	2 tsp. vanilla extract
2 cups dark brown sugar, packed	1 egg white
4 eggs, beaten	3/4 cup superfine sugar
4 cups self-rising flour	pinch cream of tartar
3/4 cup Dutch-process cocoa powder	pinch of salt
1 1/4 cups milk	2 tbsp. water

Preheat the oven to 350°F (175°C). Grease an 8-in. (20-cm.) square pan and line the base with parchment paper. Beat the margarine and brown sugar in a medium bowl until pale and creamy. In a separate bowl beat the eggs. Gradually add the eggs to the creamed mixture a little at a time, beating well between each addition. Sift in the flour and cocoa, and fold the mixture until smooth. Slowly stir in the milk and vanilla. Spoon the mixture into the pan and level the surface. Bake for 1 hour until the cake is well risen and a wooden pick inserted into the center comes out clean. Set the pan on a wire rack and cool for 10 minutes. Invert the cake onto the wire rack, remove the lining paper, and leave to cool. Combine the remaining ingredients in a bowl, beat using an electric mixer for 7 to 8 minutes, or until the mixture forms smooth peaks. Slice the cake in half down the center and sandwich together using 1/2 of the frosting. Smooth the remaining frosting over the top with a palette knife. Cut into 10 bars and serve.

Store in an airtight container for up to 2 days.

Makes 10

energy bars

see variations page 156

This is the perfect snack for an athlete who needs a burst of energy to keep going.

1 3/4 cups unsalted butter
1 cup light brown sugar
2/3 cup light corn syrup
1/3 cup raisins
5 1/3 cups rolled oats
1 tsp. ground cinnamon

1/2 cup unsalted butter
14-oz. can sweetened condensed milk
1/3 cup milk chocolate chips
1/3 cup white chocolate chips
1/3 cup pumpkin seeds
1/3 cup sunflower seeds

Preheat the oven to 400°F (200°C). Grease a 13 x 9-in. (33 x 23-cm.) baking pan and line the base with parchment paper.

Place 1 1/4 cups butter, 1/2 cup brown sugar, and the syrup in a saucepan and heat gently until melted. Add the raisins, rolled oats, and cinnamon and stir well to combine. Spoon the mixture into the prepared pan. Press down with the back of a wooden spoon and bake for 15 minutes until pale golden. Put the remaining butter and sugar in a saucepan and heat until melted. Add the condensed milk and slowly bring to a boil, stirring continuously. As soon as the mixture thickens, remove from heat and spread over the granola bars. Scatter the remaining ingredients over the caramel and allow to set for 1 hour.

Using a sharp unserrated knife, cut into 24 bars.

Makes 24

raspberry chocolate bars

see variations page 157

The kids will love these cakes combining the goodness of fresh raspberries with a crunchy pecan topping reminiscent of crumble.

3 cups all-purpose flour
1 cup plus 2 tbsp. superfine sugar
1/2 cup Dutch-process cocoa powder
3 tsp. baking powder
1/3 cup unsalted butter

2 eggs
3/4 cup milk
2/3 cup roughly chopped fresh raspberries
1 cup pecans, chopped
finely grated zest of 2 oranges

Preheat the oven to 350°F (175°C). Grease a 12 x 8-in. (30 x 20-cm.) jelly roll pan and line the base with parchment paper.

Stir together the flour, 1 cup of sugar, cocoa, and baking powder. Melt 1/4 cup of the butter in a double boiler and stir in the eggs and milk. Pour into the flour mixture and stir gently until smooth. Do not beat. Fold the raspberries, pecans, and orange zest into the mixture. Pour into the prepared pan.

Bake for 40 minutes, until a wooden pick inserted into the center comes out clean. Set the pan on a wire rack to cool. Cut into 16 slices and serve.

Store in an airtight container for up to 2 days.

Makes 16

cheesecake brownies

see variations page 158

This tasty cross between a cheesecake and a bar travels well and is the perfect dessert for a day out with the family.

6 oz. semisweet chocolate
1/2 cup unsalted butter
2 eggs
3/4 cup superfine sugar
1/2 cup plus 2 tbsp. all-purpose flour
1/2 cup self-rising flour
1/2 tsp. almond extract

7 oz. low-fat cream cheese
1/4 cup superfine sugar
2 tbsp. maple syrup
2 eggs
2 tbsp. self-rising flour
1/2 cup chopped walnuts

Preheat the oven to 350°F (175°C). Grease an 8-in. (20-cm.) square pan.

Melt the chocolate and 1/4 cup butter in a double boiler, and set aside. Beat together the eggs and sugar in a medium bowl, until smooth and creamy. Stir in the flours, almond extract, and melted chocolate. Spread 1/2 of the mixture over the base of the prepared pan.

In a separate bowl, beat together the remaining butter and last 5 ingredients and pour over the mixture in the base of the pan. Tip the second 1/2 of the chocolate mixture over the filling, covering as much as possible. Sprinkle with the chopped walnuts and bake for 30 minutes. Set the pan on a wire rack to cool. Slice into squares to serve.

Store in an airtight container for up to 3 days.

Makes 10

white chocolate fudge bars

see variations page 159

Wonderfully moist with a touch of vanilla, these white chocolate fudge bars are a change from the usual chocolate bars.

1 1/2 cups all-purpose flour
1/3 tsp. baking soda
1/2 cup unsalted butter
3 oz. white chocolate
2 eggs

2 cups superfine sugar
2 tsp. vanilla extract
1/2 cup chopped toasted hazelnuts
1/2 cup white chocolate chips

Preheat the oven to 350°F (175°C). Line a 9 x 13-in.- (23 x 33-cm.-) deep pan with parchment. Sift the flour and baking soda together in a bowl. Melt the butter and white chocolate in a heatproof bowl over a saucepan of simmering water, or in the microwave on a low heat.

In a separate bowl, beat the eggs until foamy, then beat in the sugar until well-blended. Stir in the melted chocolate, butter, and vanilla.

Add the dry ingredients and spoon into the pan. Level the surface and sprinkle with the chocolate chips. Place the pan on a baking sheet and bake for 25 to 30 minutes. Remove from the oven, allow to cool in the tray for 10 minutes, then invert onto parchment on a wire tray and cool for 30 minutes. Invert onto chopping board and cut into bars. When completely cool, store in an airtight container for 5 to 7 days.

Makes 2 dozen

variations

pecan brownies with sour cream frosting

see base recipe page 131

pistachio & pine nut brownies
Prepare the basic recipe, replacing the pecans with 1/2 cup chopped, shelled, unsalted pistachios and 2/3 cup pine nuts.

chocolate orange brownies
Prepare the basic recipe, replacing the semisweet and white chocolates with an equal quantity of orange-flavored chocolate (see page 10), and replacing the vanilla extract with 1/2 teaspoon orange oil.

chocolate & marshmallow brownie
Prepare the basic recipe, replacing the semisweet and white chocolates with an equal quantity of milk chocolate. Stir in 1 heaping cup miniature marshmallows.

chocolate, sour cherry & cranberry brownies
Prepare the basic recipe, replacing the white chocolate with semisweet chocolate, and replacing the pecans with an equal quantity of dried sour cherries and cranberries.

crunchy double choc chunk brownies
Omit the frosting. Melt 3 oz. semisweet chocolate and drizzle on top of the brownies and sprinkle with 2 tablespoons toasted sliced almonds.

millionaires' shortbread

see base recipe page 133

fruity millionaires' shortbread
Prepare the basic recipe stirring 1/3 cup raisins and 1/4 cup chopped candied cherries into the shortbread mixture.

hazelnut millionaires' shortbread
Prepare the basic recipe stirring 1/2 cup roasted chopped hazelnuts into the shortbread and replacing the semisweet chocolate with white chocolate.

chocolate–orange millionaires' shortbread
Prepare the basic recipe stirring 1 tablespoon grated orange zest into the shortbread and a couple of drops of orange extract into the caramel. Replace the semisweet chocolate with orange-flavored semisweet chocolate (see page 10).

double chocolate millionaires' shortbread
Prepare the basic recipe omitting 1/4 cup all-purpose flour and replacing with cocoa powder and stirring 1/3 cup semisweet chocolate chips into the shortbread mixture.

seeded millionaires' shortbread
Prepare the basic recipe scattering 1 cup toasted mixed pine nuts, sunflower seeds, and pumpkin seeds over the top of the melted chocolate. Allow to set.

chocolate & ginger granola bars

see base recipe page 134

white chocolate & cherry granola bars
Prepare the basic recipe, replacing the semisweet chocolate chips with white chocolate chips. Omit the ground ginger and preserved ginger, and stir in 1/2 cup chopped candied cherries.

nutty chocolate & ginger granola bars
Prepare the basic recipe, replacing 2/3 cup of rolled oats with 1/3 cup mixed pumpkin, sesame, and sunflower seeds.

white chocolate & cranberry granola bars
Prepare the basic recipe, replacing the semisweet chocolate chips with white chocolate chunks, replacing the ground ginger and ginger with 1/2 cup dried cranberries. Spread the top of the cooked granola bars with 8 oz. melted white chocolate, and leave to set.

brazil nut granola bars
Prepare the basic recipe, replacing the chocolate chips, ground ginger, and preserved ginger with 2 oz. milk chocolate chunks, roughly chopped, and 1/2 cup roughly chopped Brazil nuts.

variations

bittersweet chocolate crunchies

see base recipe page 137

chocolate raisin crunchies
Prepare the basic cookie dough and add 1/2 cup raisins to the mixture.

chocolate chip & pecan crunchies
Prepare the basic cookie dough and add 1/2 cup white chocolate chips and
1/2 cup coarsely chopped pecans to the mixture.

chocolate cherry crunchies
Prepare the basic cookie dough and add 1/2 cup chopped red candied
cherries to the mixture.

variations

chocolate-orange no-bake fruit bars

see base recipe page 138

chocolate-tropical no-bake fruit bars
Prepare the basic recipe, replacing the candied cherries and preserved ginger with 3 tablespoons each of chopped dried mango and pineapple.

spiked chocolate-orange no-bake fruit bars
Prepare the basic recipe, replacing half the orange juice with 1/4 cup orange liqueur.

chocolate-ginger no-bake fruit bars
Prepare the basic recipe, replacing the shortbread with 12 oz. gingersnaps.

muesli no-bake fruit bars
Prepare the basic recipe, replacing 4 oz. shortbread cookies with 2/3 cup granola.

rich fruit no-bake bars
Prepare the basic recipe, replacing the apricots, pistachios, and ginger with 1 cup mixed dried cherries, cranberries, and blueberries.

variations

devil's food cake bars

see base recipe page 141

coconut devil's food cake bars
Prepare the basic recipe, sprinkling the top of the cake with 1/3 cup toasted flaked coconut.

fairy princess devil's food cake bars
Prepare the basic recipe, adding a few drops of pink food coloring to the frosting. Swirl over the top of the cake and sprinkle with 1 tablespoon colored sugar.

mocha devil's food cake bars
Prepare the basic recipe, adding 1 tablespoon prepared espresso, cooled, to the frosting. Swirl over the top of the cake and decorate with walnut halves.

halloween devil's food cake bars
Prepare the basic recipe, adding a few drops of orange food coloring to the frosting. Swirl over the top of the cake and sprinkle with pumpkin-shape candies.

springtime devil's food cake bars
Prepare the basic recipe, adding a few drops of yellow food coloring to the frosting. Swirl over the top of the cake and decorate with miniature chicks.

variations

energy bars

see base recipe page 142

energy fruit bars
Prepare the basic recipe, omitting the pumpkin and sunflower seeds and scattering 1/3 cup each of raisins and chopped dried apricots over the mixture.

energy berry bars
Prepare the basic recipe, omitting the pumpkin and sunflower seeds and scattering 1/2 cup each of sour cherries, blueberries, and dried sweetened cranberries over the mixture.

energy crisp bars
Prepare the basic recipe, omitting the pumpkin and sunflower seeds and scattering 2 cups crisped rice cereal over the mixture.

nutty cluster energy fruit bars
Prepare the basic recipe, omitting the pumpkin and sunflower seeds and scattering 1/2 cup honey nut cluster breakfast cereal over the mixture.

cheerio energy bars
Prepare the basic recipe, omitting the pumpkin and sunflower seeds and scattering 1/2 cup Cheerios over the mixture.

variations

raspberry chocolate bars

see base recipe page 145

raspberry & white chocolate bars
Prepare the basic recipe, replacing the raspberries with 1 cup mandarin oranges and stirring 1/2 cup white chocolate chips into the cake mix. Melt 2 oz. white chocolate and drizzle in diagonal lines over the top of the cooled cake.

sour cherry chocolate bars
Prepare the basic recipe, replacing the raspberries with 1 cup dried sour cherries.

coconut chocolate bars
Prepare the basic recipe, replacing the raspberries with 1 1/3 cups dry flaked coconut and 1 tablespoon milk.

black cherry chocolate bars
Prepare the basic recipe, replacing the raspberries with 1 cup pitted, halved black cherries.

blackberry & almond chocolate bars
Prepare the basic recipe, replacing the raspberries with 2/3 cup fresh blackberries and the pecans with 1 1/3 cups sliced almonds.

variations

cheesecake brownies

see base recipe page 146

brazil nut cheesecake brownies
Prepare the basic recipe, replacing the chopped walnuts with 1/2 cup chopped Brazil nuts.

orange cheesecake brownies
Prepare the basic recipe, replacing the semisweet chocolate with 6 oz. orange-flavored semisweet chocolate (see page 10) and the almond extract with 1/2 teaspoon orange extract.

hazelnut cheesecake brownies
Prepare the basic recipe, replacing the chopped walnuts with 1/2 cup chopped roasted hazelnuts.

pecan cheesecake brownies
Prepare the basic recipe, replacing the chopped walnuts with 1/2 cup roughly chopped pecans.

white chocolate cheesecake brownies
Prepare the basic recipe, replacing the semisweet chocolate with 6 oz. white chocolate.

white chocolate fudge bars

see base recipe page 149

white chocolate butterscotch bars
Prepare the basic cookie dough and substitute light brown sugar for the superfine sugar and butterscotch chips for the white chocolate chips.

double chocolate fudge bars
Prepare the basic cookie dough and substitute bittersweet chocolate for the white chocolate.

chocolate cherry fudge bars
Prepare the basic cookie dough and substitute bittersweet chocolate for the white chocolate, and add 1/2 cup chopped red candied cherries.

celebration cakes

White chocolate Christmas cake, smooth praline truffle, classic black forest gateau, and creamy Easter cake — there are enough stunning cakes in this chapter to supply you with a celebration cake for every occasion.

lemon & chocolate praline cake

see variations page 182

Creamy white-chocolate frosting and crunchy praline is a delicious combination.

10 oz. white chocolate, broken into pieces
1 1/4 cups whipping cream
1 cup superfine sugar
1 cup unsalted butter
2 lemons, finely grated zest and juice

4 eggs
2 cups self-rising flour, sifted
3/4 cup whole blanched almonds
3/4 cup whole blanched hazelnuts
3/4 cup granulated sugar

Preheat the oven to 350°F (175°C). Grease and line a 8 1/2 x 4 1/2 x 2 1/2-in. loaf pan. Put the white chocolate and cream in a nonstick saucepan and heat gently until the chocolate has melted. Remove from the heat and stir until smooth. Chill in the refrigerator for 1 hour. Beat the superfine sugar, butter, lemon juice and zest in a medium bowl until pale and smooth. Add the eggs a little at a time, beating well between each addition. Fold in the flour using a large metal spoon. Spoon the mixture into the prepared pan. Bake for 1 hour, or until golden and a knife inserted into the center comes out clean. Invert on a wire rack to cool. Put the nuts and granulated sugar in a small saucepan. Heat very gently, stirring occasionally, for 5 to 10 minutes, or until the sugar dissolves and turns golden brown. Pour onto a greased cookie sheet and allow to cool. Remove the white chocolate frosting from the refrigerator and beat until soft and spreadable. Slice the cake into 3 and sandwich together using 1/2 the white chocolate frosting. Stand the cake on a dinner plate and spread the remaining frosting over the top and sides. Put the cooled praline in a plastic food bag and crush into small pieces using a rolling pin. Scatter the praline over the top and sides of the frosted cake. Store unfrosted in an airtight container for up to 2 days.

Serves 12

white chocolate christmas cake

see variations page 183

This stunning cake makes a lighter alternative to the traditional dark Christmas cake.

1 1/2 cups unsalted butter
1 tsp. vanilla extract
1 cup plus 2 tbsp. superfine sugar
5 eggs
1 1/2 cups all-purpose flour
1 1/2 cups self-rising flour
2 oranges, finely grated zest and juice
2/3 cup dried apricots, chopped
1/2 cup blanched almonds, chopped
1/2 cup roasted chopped hazelnuts

1 3/4 cups confectioners' sugar
2 tbsp. orange liqueur
1 lemon, finely grated zest and juice
3 tbsp. apricot jam
1 lb. white marzipan
1 lb. white chocolate
4 oz. semisweet chocolate
1/2 cup candied peel
12 green seedless grapes
6 dried apricots

Preheat the oven to 350°F (175°C). Grease and line an 8-in. (20-cm.) round deep cake pan. Beat together 1 cup butter, vanilla, and sugar in a bowl until pale and creamy. Beat in the eggs, one at a time, beating well between each addition. Sift in the flours and gently fold into the cake mixture, along with 3 tablespoons orange juice and 1 tablespoon grated zest. Fold in the apricots, almonds, and hazelnuts and spoon into the prepared pan. Bake for 1 hour. Cover with aluminum foil and cook for 30 minutes more, until well risen and a wooden pick inserted into the center comes out clean. Set the pan on a wire rack to cool. Invert the cake onto a dinner plate and using a sharp knife level the surfaces. Put the remaining 1/2 cup butter, confectioners' sugar, orange liqueur, and lemon zest and juice into a bowl and beat until light and creamy. Using a sharp knife, slice the cake in half. Sandwich the 2 halves together with the buttercream. Heat the apricot jam in a saucepan and use to brush over the

top and sides of the cake. Knead the marzipan on a surface lightly dusted with confectioners' sugar and roll out thinly. Use to cover the top and sides of the cake and smooth with the palms of your hands. Melt the white chocolate in a double boiler. Remove from the heat and allow to cool for 5 minutes. Set the cake on a wire rack above a tray. Pour over the melted chocolate until the top and sides are coated evenly. Allow to set for 2 hours. Melt the semisweet chocolate in a double boiler. Cut the candied peel into strips and dip into the melted chocolate. Half-dip the grapes and apricots in the chocolate. When the chocolate has set, arrange the peel and fruit on top of the cake. Transfer to a dinner plate to serve.

Serves 12–16

almond gateau

see variations page 184

This cake slices beautifully making it ideal to serve as part of a celebratory meal.

1 cup ground almonds
1 cup plus 1 tbsp. superfine sugar
8 eggs
1/2 cup plus 2 tbsp. self-rising flour
1/4 cup granulated sugar
1/4 cup water
1 cup light cream

1 cup plus 2 tbsp. unsalted butter
1/3 cup confectioners' sugar
2 tbsp. instant coffee granules
2 1/2 oz. semisweet chocolate, melted
2 tbsp. Dutch-process cocoa powder
8 oz. white almond paste
confectioners' sugar to dust
fresh mint leaves, to decorate

Preheat the oven to 375°F (190°C). Grease and line an 8-in. (20-cm.) square cake pan. Stir together the almonds and 1/2 cup superfine sugar. Beat in 4 eggs, one at a time. Sift in the flour and fold gently. Separate the remaining 4 eggs. Put the egg whites in a bowl and beat with an electric mixer until stiff peaks form. Fold in 1 tablespoon superfine sugar. Lightly fold the egg whites into the cake batter. Spoon the batter into the prepared pan and bake for 35 minutes, or until firm. Remove from the oven and invert on a wire rack to cool. Put the granulated sugar in a saucepan with the water. Bring to a boil and simmer for 2 minutes. Set aside to cool. Beat the remaining 1/2 cup superfine sugar and 4 egg yolks in a bowl until pale and smooth. Bring the cream to a boil in a small saucepan, then add to the egg mixture. Beat to combine. Return the mixture to a clean saucepan and cook over a low heat for 2 minutes until it begins to thicken. Pour through a strainer and set aside to cool completely. Beat the butter in a bowl until softened. Gradually add the cooled mixture

and confectioners' sugar and beat well to combine. Divide the buttercream in half. Dissolve the coffee in 1 tablespoon boiling water and beat into one half of the buttercream. Beat the melted chocolate into the other half. Chill in the refrigerator for 30 minutes. Slice the cake into 3 layers. Drizzle each layer with a little syrup, then sandwich together using the chocolate buttercream. Using a palette knife, spread the coffee buttercream over the top and sides of the cake. Chill for 30 minutes in the refrigerator before dusting the cake with 1 tablespoon cocoa. Knead the remaining cocoa into the almond paste. Roll out thinly on a surface lightly dusted with confectioners' sugar. Cut into long strips, 1 1/2-in. (4-cm.) wide and arrange in ruffles on top of the cake. Dust lightly with confectioners' sugar and decorate with mint leaves to serve. The syrups and buttercreams can be made up to 2 days in advance. To soften the buttercream for use leave at room temperature for 30 minutes before beating well. Almond paste dries out quickly so work fast when kneading the cocoa into it.

Serves 12

easter cake

see variations page 185

This cake sinks a little during baking, however the delightful decoration disguises this.

1 1/3 cups confectioners' sugar
1/2 cup Dutch-process cocoa powder
1/2 cup hot water
2 cups roasted ground hazelnuts
6 eggs, separated

1/2 cup superfine sugar
4 oz. semisweet chocolate
1 1/4 cups whipping cream
8 oz. white chocolate
12 miniature chocolate eggs

Preheat the oven to 350°F (175°C). Grease and line the base of two 8-in. (20-cm.) deep-sided round pans. Sift the confectioners' sugar and cocoa into a bowl and stir in the hot water and hazelnuts. In a separate bowl, beat the egg whites with an electric mixer until stiff. Beat in the superfine sugar, a little at a time, until the mixture is smooth and glossy. Fold the egg whites into the cocoa mixture using a large metal spoon and a figure 8 movement. Divide the mixture between the pans and bake for 20 minutes until well risen and firm. Set the pans onto wire racks to cool. Put the semisweet chocolate and cream in a saucepan and melt over a low heat. Remove from the heat and beat for 2 to 3 minutes until smooth. Chill in the refrigerator for 30 minutes. Beat again to soften, then use to sandwich the cakes together. Melt the white chocolate in a double boiler. Pour onto a cookie sheet lined with parchment paper and allow to set. Beat the remaining cream with an electric mixer until soft peaks form, and spread over the top and sides of the cake. Using a sharp knife, draw the blade across the set chocolate on the cookie sheet to form chocolate curls. Coat the top and sides of the cake with the curls and decorate with the chocolate eggs. The cake can be baked up to 1 day in advance, but it is best assembled on the day it is to be served.

Serves 12

praline truffle

see variations page 186

When making the praline, keep an eye on the sugar as it cooks and browns very quickly.

1/2 cup superfine sugar
1 cup whole blanched almonds
1 lb. 2 oz. semisweet chocolate
1 1/2 cups whipping cream

2/3 cup unsalted butter
1 tbsp. rum
confectioners' sugar to dust

Grease and line the base of a 8 1/2 x 4 1/2 x 2 1/2-in. loaf pan. Grease a cookie sheet. Put the sugar and almonds in a small saucepan and cook over a low heat until the sugar has melted. Cook for 1 minute until it turns a pale golden brown. Pour the almond praline onto the cookie sheet and allow to cool completely. Melt all but 4 oz. of the chocolate in a double boiler. Remove from heat and leave to cool. Put the praline in a plastic food bag and crush with a rolling pin. Whisk the cream with an electric mixer until soft peaks form. In a separate bowl, beat the butter until light and then add the cooled chocolate and rum and beat to combine. Fold in the whipped cream and praline then spoon the mixture into the prepared pan. Leave to set for 3 to 4 hours, or overnight.

Melt the remaining chocolate and spread onto a parchment paper-lined cookie sheet. Allow to set completely. Using a sharp knife, draw the blade at an angle across the chocolate to form curls and ruffles. Run a warm knife around the edge of the cake pan and invert the cake onto a dinner plate. Pile the chocolate curls on top, dust lightly with confectioners' sugar, and serve.

Serves 12

nutty chocolate meringue

see variations page 187

This nutty meringue deserves to be served at the end of a special meal.

1/2 cup Dutch-process cocoa powder
1 1/3 cups confectioners' sugar
10 eggs
2/3 cup granulated sugar
1/4 cup walnut halves, roughly chopped
1/4 cup pistachio nuts, roughly chopped
10 oz. semisweet chocolate

1/3 cup unsalted butter
3 tbsp. orange liqueur
2 tbsp. superfine sugar
2/3 cup fromage frais or mascarpone
2/3 cup unflavored yogurt
1 tbsp. orange juice

Preheat the oven to 275°F (140°C). Line 3 cookie sheets with parchment paper and draw an 8-in. (20-cm.) diameter circle in the center of each. Sift the cocoa and confectioners' sugar into a bowl. In a large bowl, separate 6 eggs and discard the yolks. Beat the egg whites with an electric mixer until stiff peaks form. Gradually beat in the granulated sugar, 1 tablespoon at a time, until the mixture is thick and glossy. Using a large metal spoon fold in the sifted cocoa and confectioners' sugar until the meringue is evenly colored. Spoon half of the meringue between the 2 circles and spread out evenly using a palette knife. Scatter a third of the nuts over each meringue. Spoon the remaining meringue into a large frosting bag fitted with a large star nozzle. Pipe rows of meringue in a wave pattern across the remaining circle until it is completely covered. Scatter with the remaining nuts. Cook the meringues for 1 1/2 hours until pale brown and completely dry to the touch. Set on a wire rack to cool completely before removing the parchment paper.

Melt the chocolate in a double boiler. Remove from the heat. Separate the remaining 4 eggs and add the yolks, butter, and 2 tablespoons orange liqueur to the chocolate and stir well until smooth. Set aside to cool. Beat the egg whites with an electric mixer until stiff peaks form. Add the superfine sugar and beat until slightly glossy. Fold the egg whites into the cooled chocolate. Chill in the refrigerator for 20 minutes. Put one of the meringues onto a dinner plate, flat side down. Using 2 dessert spoons, shape quenelles of chocolate mousse around the outside edge of the meringue. Fill the center of the mousse ring with more chocolate mousse and top with the second disc of meringue. Repeat with the remaining mousse before topping with the piped meringue disc. Chill in the refrigerator for up to 6 hours. Beat together the remaining ingredients to create the sauce, and serve on the side. The meringue can be made up to 1 week in advance and stored in an airtight container. The mousse and sauce should be prepared the day the cake is served.

Serves 10

classic black forest gateau

see variations page 188

This cake is decorated with chocolate leaves that look fabulous but are easy to make.

4 eggs
1/2 cup superfine sugar
3/4 cup all-purpose flour, sifted
1/4 cup Dutch-process cocoa powder, sifted
3 tbsp. Kirsch or Framboise
12 oz. white chocolate, broken into pieces

4 oz. semisweet chocolate, broken into pieces
15-20 washed rose leaves
2 1/2 cups whipping cream
3/4 20-oz. can red cherry pie filling
confectioners' sugar to dust
fresh mint leaves, to decorate

Preheat the oven to 375°F (190°C). Grease and line an 8-in. (20-cm.) springform pan. Put the eggs and superfine sugar in a bowl and beat until pale and smooth. Add the flour and cocoa and fold in gently. Spoon into the prepared pan and cook for 25 to 30 minutes, or until the cake springs back when pressed with the fingertips. Set the pan on a wire rack to cool. Slice horizontally into 4 equal layers, drizzle a little Kirsch over each layer, and set aside. Melt the white chocolate in a double boiler. Spread the white chocolate onto a parchment paper-lined cookie sheet and allow to set. Using a sharp knife, draw the blade, at an angle across the white chocolate to form curls and ruffles. Place the semisweet chocolate in a double boiler. When melted, paint the chocolate thickly on the underside of each rose leaf and allow to set. Whisk the cream with an electric mixer until soft peaks form. Spoon 1/4 into a frosting bag fitted with a large star nozzle, and set 2 tablespoons of cherry pie filling aside. Sandwich the

cake layers together with 2/3 the remaining cream and the rest of the cherry pie filling. Stand the cake on a dinner plate and spread the remaining 1/3 of the cream round the sides. Pat the white chocolate curls over the cream to cover completely and pipe rosettes of cream round the top of the cake. Spoon a little pie filling over each. Carefully peel away the rose leaves from the chocolate shapes. Decorate the cake with the chocolate leaves and mint leaves and dust with confectioners' sugar just before serving. Chill in the refrigerator until required. This cake is best eaten on the same day.

Serves 10-12

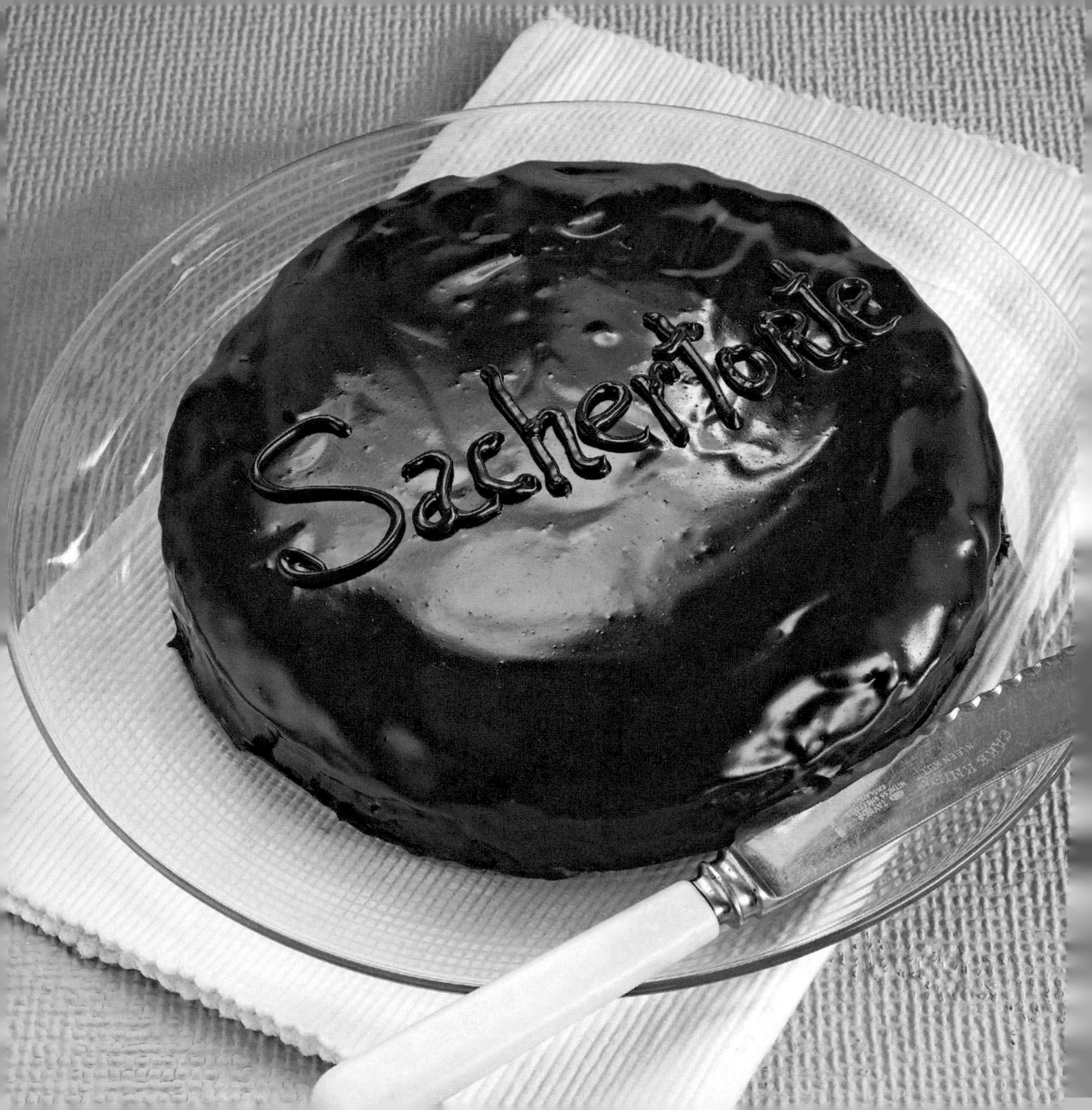
Sachertorte

sachertorte

see variations page 189

The original recipe was devised in Vienna in 1832 and kept a closely guarded secret!

6 oz. semisweet chocolate
2/3 cup unsalted butter
1/2 cup superfine sugar
3 large eggs, separated
1 1/4 cups all-purpose flour
1 tbsp. water

1/3 cup apricot jam
6 oz. semisweet chocolate, at least
    50% cocoa solids
2/3 cup whipping cream
2 tsp. food-grade glycerin, optional (from cake
    decorating stores or wine-making supply stores)

Preheat the oven to 350°F (175°C). Grease a 9-in. (23-cm.) springform pan. Melt the chocolate in a double boiler. Set aside to cool for 30 minutes. Beat the butter and sugar in a bowl until creamy. Beat in the egg yolks, one at a time, beating well after each addition. Fold in the cooled chocolate. In a separate bowl, beat the egg whites with an electric mixer until stiff. Lightly fold into the chocolate mixture using a large metal spoon. Sift in the flour, add the water, and fold in. Spoon the mixture into the pan and bake for 30 minutes until well risen. Remove from the oven and transfer to a wire rack to cool completely. Slice the cake in half and sandwich together using 1/2 the jam. Set on a wire rack over a tray. Warm the remaining jam in a saucepan and brush over the top and sides of the cake. Allow to set for 30 minutes. Put the chocolate and cream in a double boiler and heat until melted. Remove from the heat, add the glycerin, and stir until smooth. Reserve 1 tablespoon of sauce and pour the remaining sauce over the cake so that it covers the top and sides completely. Do this in one movement so the frosting is perfectly smooth. Spoon the remaining frosting into a frosting bag fitted with a small plain nozzle and pipe the word "sachertorte" across the top. Allow to cool for 2 to 3 hours. Store unfrosted for up to 3 days.

Serves 10-12

chocolate & almond strudel

see variations page 190

This wickedly sticky strudel will have everyone asking for seconds.

3 eggs
1/3 cup superfine sugar
1 1/3 cups ground almonds
1/2 tsp. almond extract
1 cup sliced almonds or chopped mixed nuts

6 large sheets of phyllo dough
1/4 cup unsalted butter, melted
4 oz. semisweet chocolate, grated
1 1/4 cups whipping cream
4 oz. semisweet chocolate, broken into pieces

Preheat the oven to 350°F (175°C). Put the eggs, sugar, almonds, and almond extract in a food processor and process until well combined. Stir in the sliced almonds. Lay a sheet of phyllo dough on the countertop and brush lightly with melted butter. Lay a second sheet on top and brush with butter. Repeat with a third sheet of phyllo. Brush with butter and sprinkle with half the grated chocolate. Lay a fourth sheet on top and brush with butter. Repeat with a fifth, and then a sixth sheet, each time brushing with butter. Spread the almond mixture across a third of the last phyllo sheet, then sprinkle the remaining chocolate across the whole sheet. Gently roll up the strudel.

Lift onto a parchment paper-lined cookie sheet and brush with extra melted butter. Cook for 25 to 30 minutes until crisp and golden.

Put the cream in a saucepan and bring to a boil. Remove from the heat and add the chocolate. When the chocolate has melted, stir until smooth. Transfer the strudel to a dinner plate, pour over the chocolate, and serve.

Serves 6

fudgy chocolate pudding

see variations page 191

From the pantry to the oven in less than 5 minutes

2 cups light brown sugar, packed
3/4 cup self-rising flour
1 tsp. baking powder
3/4 cup Dutch-process cocoa powder

4 eggs, beaten
1 cup unsalted butter, melted
1 tsp. vanilla extract
1 cup roasted chopped hazelnuts

Preheat the oven to 325°F (160°C). Grease a 9-in. (23-cm.) deep-dish pie plate.

Put all the ingredients in a large bowl and beat well with a wooden spoon until well combined and evenly colored.

Pour the mixture into the plate and stand the plate in the center of a large roasting pan. Half fill with the pan with boiling water and bake for 1 hour or until well risen and firm.

Serve warm with cream or ice cream. Can be served cold cut into squares.

Serves 8

hot chocolate soufflé

see variations page 192

This wonderful dessert will sink before your eyes if made to wait, so make sure your guests are ready and serve it straight from the oven.

superfine sugar, for coating cups
4 oz. white chocolate
4 oz. semisweet chocolate
1/4 cup superfine sugar

3 large eggs, separated
1/4 tsp. vanilla extract
confectioners' sugar, for dusting

Freeze the white chocolate for 15 minutes. Preheat the oven to 400°F (200°C). Generously butter and four 5-fl. oz. (125-ml.) ceramic baking cups. Half fill one baking cup with superfine sugar and swirl around to coat the inside. Pour the sugar into the next cup and repeat until all 4 cups are coated.

Melt the semisweet chocolate in a double boiler. Using an electric mixer, beat together the superfine sugar, egg yolks, and vanilla until pale and smooth. Remove the melted chocolate from the heat and stir into the creamed egg mixture. In a separate bowl beat the egg whites with an electric mixer until stiff peaks form. Fold 1/2 the egg whites into the chocolate mixture, using a large metal spoon and a figure 8 movement. Fold in the remaining egg whites, folding until the mixture is an even color.

Put 1/8 of the mixture in each cup. Top with a piece of chilled white chocolate and then fill the cups with the remaining mixture. Bake for 15 minutes or until well risen and slightly spongy around the edges. Dust with confectioners' sugar and serve immediately.

Serves 4

layered birthday cookie

see variations page 193

Create your own extravagant birthday alternative for a cookie lover.

for the cookie
1 cup unsalted butter
2 cups light brown sugar
2 eggs
2 tsp. vanilla extract
3 cups all-purpose flour
6 tbsp. Dutch process cocoa powder
1 tsp. baking soda

for the topping
1/2 cup unsalted butter
2 cups confectioners' sugar
1 cup cream cheese
1 cup melted bittersweet chocolate
1/2 cup candies
1/2 cup semisweet chocolate chips

Preheat the oven to 350°F (175°C). Line two 11-in. (28-cm.) springform pans with parchment.

Beat the butter and sugar together. Add the eggs and vanilla extract. Sift the flour, cocoa powder, and baking soda and stir into the batter. Divide the dough in two, and press into the prepared pans. Bake for 20 minutes until golden. Remove from the oven and allow to cool, then transfer to a wire rack.

To prepare the topping, beat the butter and confectioners' sugar together, then beat in the cream cheese and melted chocolate. Spread the topping over the cooled cookies, place one on top of the other, decorate, and top with chocolate chips and candies.

Makes 1 large cookie

lemon & chocolate praline cake

see base recipe page 161

orange & chocolate praline cake
Prepare the basic recipe, replacing the lemons with oranges and the white chocolate with 8 oz. milk chocolate.

amaretti, lemon & chocolate praline cake
Prepare the basic recipe, replacing the praline mixture with 10 crushed amaretti.

double lemon & chocolate praline cake
Prepare the basic recipe. Spread two of the cake layers each with 2 tablespoons of lemon curd before spreading and sandwiching together with the white chocolate buttercream.

lemon & semisweet chocolate praline cake
Prepare the basic recipe, replacing the white chocolate with 10 oz. semisweet chocolate.

orange & milk chocolate praline cake
Prepare the basic recipe, replacing the white chocolate with 10 oz. milk chocolate and replacing the lemons with 2 oranges.

white chocolate christmas cake

see base recipe page 162

dark chocolate christmas cake
Prepare the basic recipe, replacing the white chocolate with 1 lb. unsweetened dark chocolate.

macadamia nut & chocolate christmas cake
Prepare the basic recipe, replacing the almonds and hazelnuts with 1 cup chopped macadamia nuts.

spiked chocolate christmas cake
Prepare the basic recipe, soaking the apricots in 2 tablespoons brandy for 10 minutes before using and drizzling 1 tablespoon brandy over the top of each cake half before sandwiching together with buttercream.

orange chocolate christmas cake
Prepare the basic recipe, replacing the white chocolate with 1 lb. orange-flavored semisweet chocolate (see page 10).

white chocolate truffle christmas cake
Prepare the basic recipe, omitting the candied peel and fruit. Arrange 1 lb. assorted chocolate truffles and chocolates around the edge of the cake and use the remaining melted chocolate to make chocolate rose leaves. Arrange between the truffles and serve.

almond gateau

see base recipe page 164

orange & almond gateau
Prepare the basic recipe, stirring 1 tablespoon of finely grated orange zest and 1 tablespoon of orange juice into the batter.

espresso & almond gateau
Prepare the basic recipe, stirring 2 tablespoons prepared espresso, cooled, into the batter. Omit the almond paste and decorate with chocolate-coated coffee beans.

double almond gateau
Prepare the basic recipe. Omit the almond paste and cocoa and pat the top and sides of the cake with 1 cup chopped praline (use recipe on page 168).

hazelnut & almond gateau
Prepare the basic recipe, replacing ground almonds with 3/4 cup ground roasted hazelnuts.

almond christmas gateau
Prepare the basic recipe. Instead of making chocolate ruffles, roll out the chocolate almond paste thinly and stamp out a selection of leaf shapes using cutters. Mark veins with a sharp knife and arrange the leaves in a wreath shape on the top of the cake before decorating with a ribbon bow to serve.

variations

easter cake

see base recipe page 167

white summer chocolate cake
Prepare the basic recipe. Omit the chocolate eggs and decorate with
12 semisweet chocolate-dipped strawberries.

marbled easter cake
Prepare the basic recipe. Replace half the white chocolate with 4 oz. milk
chocolate and use to make milk chocolate curls. Stir the white and milk
chocolate curls together and continue as per recipe.

almond easter cake
Prepare the basic recipe. Replace the hazelnuts with 2 1/3 cups ground
almonds and stir 1/2 teaspoon almond extract into the cake mixture.

gluten-free easter cake
Prepare the basic recipe omitting the cocoa and replacing with an equal
quantity of equivalent gluten-free cocoa products (see page 10).

chocolate truffle birthday cake
Prepare the basic recipe. Omit the chocolate eggs and decorate with
20 chocolate truffles.

variations

praline truffle

see base recipe page 168

praline cherry truffle
Prepare the basic recipe, adding 1/2 cup chopped candied cherries and
replacing the semisweet chocolate with an equal quantity of milk chocolate.

praline & shortbread truffle
Prepare the basic recipe, stirring 3/4 cup broken shortbread cookies into the
truffle cake mixture.

berry & praline truffle
Prepare the basic recipe, stirring 1 cup chopped mixed dried cranberries and
blueberries into the truffle cake mixture.

light & dark praline truffle
Prepare the basic recipe, replacing 7 oz. of the semisweet chocolate with
7 oz. white chocolate. Divide the beaten cream mixture in half and fold
white chocolate into one half and the semisweet chocolate into the other.
Add the praline. Spoon the white chocolate truffle onto the cookie sheet
followed by the semisweet chocolate truffle.

dairy-free praline truffle
Prepare the basic recipe omitting the semisweet chocolate, cream, and
butter and replacing with equivalent dairy-free products (see page 10).

variations

nutty chocolate meringue

see base recipe page 170

double orange nutty chocolate meringue
Prepare the basic recipe, replacing the semisweet chocolate with 10 oz.
orange-flavored semisweet chocolate (see page 10).

almond chocolate meringue
Prepare the basic recipe, replacing the walnuts and pistachios with 2/3 cup
ground roasted almonds.

fresh orange & chocolate meringue
Prepare the basic recipe. Segment 2 oranges and roughly chop. Sprinkle the
chopped orange pieces on top of the chocolate mousse when assembling
the dessert. Decorate the top with grated orange zest.

nutty raspberry chocolate meringue
Prepare the basic recipe. Top the 2 meringue discs with the filling and
arrange 2/3 cup fresh raspberries over each. Proceed with recipe.

white chocolate meringue
Prepare the basic recipe omitting the semisweet chocolate and replacing
with 10 oz. white chocolate.

variations

classic black forest gateau

see base recipe page 172

mixed berry chocolate gateau
Prepare the basic recipe, replacing the cherry pie filling with 3/4 of a 20-oz. can of mixed berry pie filling.

apricot chocolate gateau
Prepare the basic recipe, replacing the cherry pie filling with 3/4 of a 20-oz. can of apricot pie filling.

mango chocolate gateau
Prepare the basic recipe, replacing the cherry pie filling with 3/4 of a drained 20-oz. can of sliced mango. Drizzle 1 tablespoon white rum over each layer of cake before assembling.

raspberry chocolate gateau
Prepare the basic recipe, replacing the cherry pie filling with 3/4 of a drained 20-oz. can of raspberries or 1 1/3 cups fresh raspberries. Drizzle 1 tablespoon framboise or cassis liqueur over each layer of cake before assembling.

black & blueberry chocolate gateau
Prepare the basic recipe, replacing the cherry pie filling with 1 1/3 cups mixed fresh blackberries and blueberries. Drizzle 1 tablespoon cassis liqueur over each layer of cake before assembling.

variations

sachertorte

see base recipe page 175

strawberry milk chocolate sachertorte
Prepare the basic recipe, replacing the apricot jam with seedless or sieved strawberry jam and the semisweet chocolate with 6 oz. milk chocolate.

orange chocolate sachertorte
Prepare the basic recipe, replacing the apricot jam with rind-less orange marmalade and the semisweet chocolate with 6 oz. orange-flavored semisweet chocolate (see page 10).

praline chocolate sachertorte
Prepare the basic recipe, stirring 3 tablespoons of fine praline (use the praline recipe on page 168) into the frosting. Omit piping "sachertorte."

ruffle sachertorte
Prepare the basic recipe, omit piping "sachertorte." Using 4 oz. each of white and semisweet chocolate, make chocolate shavings. Arrange the shavings on top of the cake.

milk chocolate & violet sachertorte
Prepare the basic recipe, replacing the semisweet chocolate with milk chocolate. Omit piping "sachertorte" and decorate with candied violets.

variations

chocolate & almond strudel

see base recipe page 176

orange & almond chocolate strudel
Prepare the basic recipe replacing the semisweet chocolate with milk chocolate. Stir 1 tablespoon finely grated orange zest into the almond mixture and omit the almond extract.

pistachio & almond chocolate strudel
Prepare the basic recipe, replacing the sliced almonds with 1 cup coarsely chopped pistachios.

frosted chocolate & almond strudel
Prepare the basic recipe. Mix together 2/3 cup confectioners' sugar and enough orange juice to form a smooth frosting. Melt 2 oz. semisweet chocolate. Drizzle the chocolate and the frosting randomly over the top of the strudel and sprinkle with 3 tablespoons sliced almonds. Allow to set.

coconut & chocolate strudel
Prepare the basic recipe, replacing the almonds and almond extract with 1 1/4 cup dry flaked coconut.

almond & apricot chocolate strudel
Prepare the basic recipe replacing the chopped mixed nuts with 2/3 cup chopped apricots.

fudgy chocolate pudding

see base recipe page 178

double fudge chocolate pudding
Prepare the basic recipe, replacing the hazelnuts with 5 small, soft
fudge pieces.

almond chocolate pudding
Prepare the basic recipe, replacing the hazelnuts with 1 1/4 cups almonds
and replacing the vanilla with 1 teaspoon almond extract.

raisin & chocolate pudding
Soak 2/3 cup raisins in 3 tablespoons orange juice for 15 minutes.
Prepare the basic recipe, replacing the hazelnuts and vanilla extract
with the soaked raisins.

gluten-free fudgy chocolate pudding
Prepare the basic recipe, omitting the self-rising flour, baking powder,
and cocoa and replacing with an equal quantity of equivalent
gluten-free products (see page 10).

variations

hot chocolate soufflé

see base recipe page 179

hot chocolate orange soufflé
Prepare the basic recipe, replacing the semisweet chocolate with 4 oz. of
the finest quality orange-flavored unsweetened chocolate (see page 10) and
replacing the vanilla extract with 1/4 teaspoon orange oil.

hot mint chocolate soufflé
Prepare the basic recipe, replacing the semisweet chocolate with 4 oz.
finest quality mint-flavored unsweetened chocolate (see page 10) and
omitting the vanilla extract.

hot chocolate caramel soufflé
Prepare the basic recipe, replacing the semisweet chocolate with 4 oz.
caramel chocolate and replacing the superfine sugar with light brown sugar.

raspberry & chocolate soufflé
Prepare the basic recipe, replacing the white chocolate with 4 teaspoons
raspberry jam and 4 fresh raspberries. Sift with confectioners' sugar.

white chocolate soufflé
Prepare the basic recipe, replacing the semisweet chocolate with 4 oz. white
chocolate, and the 4 squares of white chocolate with 4 small pieces of white
chocolate with nougat. Sift with confectioners' sugar.

layered birthday cookie

see base recipe page 180

marshmallow layered cookie
Prepare the basic cookie dough and substitute 1 cup pink marshmallow icing for the cream cheese and bittersweet chocolate and miniature marshmallows for the candies and chocolate chips.

fresh & fruity cookie cake
Prepare the basic cookie dough, omitting the cocoa powder. Substitute 2 cups heavy cream for all of the filling ingredients. Whip and sweeten the heavy cream with 2 teaspoons vanilla extract and 2 tablespoons confectioners' sugar. Spread the cream on top of the cookies and top both with fresh halved strawberries, raspberries, and blueberries.

pastries, tarts & cheesecakes

These irresistible tarts, delicious pastries, and enticing cheesecakes take a little longer to prepare, but the end results are more than worth the extra effort. You'll be asked to make these recipes time and time again.

chocolate baklava

see variations page 211

These traditional nutty pastries are a feature of Greek, Cypriot, and Turkish cuisine.

1 cup walnuts, chopped
1 cup pistachios, chopped
1/4 cup superfine sugar
1/2 tsp. ground cinnamon
3 oz. semisweet chocolate, finely chopped
1/3 cup unsalted butter, melted

7 large sheets phyllo dough
1/3 cup superfine sugar
2/3 cup water
3 tbsp. honey
finely grated zest of 1 orange

Preheat the oven to 350°F (175°C). Butter an 8-in. (20-cm.) square cake pan.

Put the nuts, sugar, cinnamon, and chocolate into a bowl and stir well. Cut the sheets of phyllo dough in half. Lightly butter 5 squares and lay one on top of the other. Lift into the pan, draping the excess pastry over the edge of the pan. Sprinkle the pastry with 1/3 of the nut mixture. Butter and stack 3 more phyllo sheets and lay over the top of the nut mixture. Repeat this twice more. Fold under any excess pastry to neaten. With a sharp knife, cut the pastry into 16 squares. Brush the top with extra butter and bake for 45 minutes, until golden brown.

Remove from the oven and cool for 5 minutes. Put the remaining ingredients in a saucepan and heat gently until melted. Bring to a boil and simmer for 2 to 3 minutes until it is syrupy. Pass through a strainer and cool for 5 minutes. Pour over the warm baklava and allow to cool completely.

Makes 16

marzipan & chocolate braid

see variations page 212

This wonderful fruity bread is delicious served for breakfast.

2 cups white bread flour
1/2 tsp. salt
1/3 cup plus 3 tbsp. unsalted butter
1 tbsp. rapid rise yeast
5 tbsp. superfine sugar
1 egg, beaten
6 tbsp. warm milk

1/2 cup chopped, dried apricots
1/2 cup milk chocolate chunks
1 tbsp. finely grated orange zest
2 oz. white marzipan, grated
1/2 cup confectioners' sugar, sifted
1–2 tbsp. fresh orange juice
1 tbsp. sliced almonds, toasted

Put the flour and salt in a bowl and cut in 3 tablespoons butter. Stir in the yeast, 2 tablespoons sugar, egg, and enough of the milk to make a soft dough. Turn out onto a surface lightly dusted with flour and knead for 10 minutes until the dough is smooth and elastic. Roll out to a 12 x 8-in. (30 x 18-cm.) rectangle. Beat the remaining butter and 3 tablespoons sugar together in a medium bowl until smooth. Stir in the apricots, chocolate chunks, and grated orange zest. Spread the mixture evenly over the dough and sprinkle with the grated marzipan. Roll up the dough from one short end like a jelly roll. Gently roll it backward and forward until the roll is approximately 14 in. (35 cm.) long. Using a sharp knife, cut the roll lengthwise into 3 long strips of equal width, leaving them joined at the top. Braid the 3 strips together, pinch the ends, and lift onto a parchment paper-lined

cookie sheet. Cover loosely with a sheet of oiled plastic wrap and leave in a warm place until doubled in size. Preheat the oven to 400°F (200°C). Bake for 10 minutes. Lower the temperature to 325°F (160°C), cover with aluminum foil, and bake for 15 minutes more, until well risen and golden brown. Combine the confectioners' sugar with enough orange juice to form a smooth, thick frosting. Drizzle over the hot braid and sprinkle with the almonds. Serve and eat while still warm.

Serves 8-10

brownie tart

see variations page 213

This tart elevates the brownie from snack food to a sophisticated dessert.

1/2 cup all-purpose flour
1/2 tsp. baking powder
1/2 tsp. salt
3 oz. unsweetened chocolate
1/3 cup unsalted butter

1 cup granulated sugar
2 large eggs, lightly beaten
1 tsp. vanilla extract
1/2 cup fresh raspberries

Preheat the oven to 350°F (175°C).

In a bowl combine the flour, baking powder, and salt. Set aside.

In a medium saucepan, melt the chocolate and butter over low heat, stirring to combine. Remove from the heat and stir in the sugar, eggs, and vanilla. Add the flour mixture and stir until just combined. Turn the mixture into a greased 9 1/2-in. (24-cm.) tart pan and bake for 20 minutes. Transfer to a wire rack to cool.

Garnish with fresh raspberries and serve with whipped cream.

Serves 6–8

pecan tart

see variations page 214

This gooey dessert is begging to be served with scoops of real vanilla ice cream and is at its very best eaten warm from the oven.

1 1/2 cups all-purpose flour, sifted
1/4 cup Dutch-process cocoa powder
2/3 cup unsalted butter, cubed
1/2 cup ground almonds
1/3 cup confectioners' sugar
1 egg yolk
2-3 tbsp. cold water
2/3 cup light brown sugar

1/2 cup unsalted butter
3 tbsp. maple syrup
3 tbsp. light corn syrup
2 eggs, beaten
1/2 tsp. vanilla extract
1/4 cup raisins
1 cup pecans

Preheat the oven to 400°F (200°C). Put the flour, cocoa, 2/3 cup butter, almonds, and confectioners' sugar in a food processor and process until the mixture resembles coarse meal. Add the egg yolk and 1 tablespoon water and process until the mixture forms a soft, but not sticky, dough. Add a little more water if necessary. Wrap in plastic wrap and chill in the refrigerator for 30 minutes. Using a rolling pin, thinly roll out the pastry on a surface lightly dusted with flour and use to line a 14 1/2 x 4 1/2-in. (36 x 12-cm.) tranche pan. Prick the base and bake blind for 10 minutes. Lower the temperature to 300°F (150°C). Put the brown sugar, butter, and syrups in a saucepan, and heat gently until melted. Allow to cool for 5 minutes, then stir in the eggs, vanilla, raisins, and pecans. Pour the mixture into the pastry case and bake for 45 minutes or until just firm to the touch. Serve warm.

Serves 8-10

unsweetend chocolate & raspberry tartlets

see variations page 215

Naughty but oh so nice. These individual tartlets look great when piled on a tray.

2/3 cup unsalted butter, cubed
2 tbsp. superfine sugar
1 egg yolk
2 cups all-purpose flour, sifted
1 1/4 cups whipping cream

10 oz. unsweetened chocolate
2 eggs, separated
2 tbsp. rum
2 2/3 cups raspberries, washed
3 tbsp. redcurrant jelly

Preheat the oven to 400°F (200°C). Put the butter, sugar, and egg yolk in a food processor and process until smooth. Add the flour and process until just combined. Do not over-process or the pastry will be tough. Turn onto a lightly floured surface and knead very gently until smooth and soft. Wrap and chill in the refrigerator for 30 minutes. Before use, remove the pastry from the refrigerator to return to room temperature. Roll out the pastry on a surface lightly dusted with flour. Cut 8 discs using a 3 1 /2-in. (9-cm.) cookie cutter and use to line 8 loose-based tartlet pans. Bake blind for 10 minutes. Remove the beans, or pie weights, and paper and bake for 5 minutes more. Allow to cool in the pans and set aside. Lower the temperature to 375°F (190°C). Put the cream and chocolate in a nonstick saucepan and heat gently until the chocolate has melted. Remove from the heat and allow to cool. Beat the egg whites using an electric mixer until stiff peaks form. Stir the rum and yolks into the melted chocolate before gently folding in the egg whites. Divide the mixture between the 8

pastry cups and bake for 10 minutes until just set. Allow to cool in the pans. Transfer to the refrigerator to chill for 3 hours or overnight. Remove the tartlets from the pans and top each with raspberries. Melt the redcurrant jelly with 1 tablespoon water in a saucepan. Drizzle a little of the glaze over each tart. Serve warm or cold.

Makes 8

baked maple–pecan cheesecake

see variations page 216

The cookies can be easily crushed in a food processor but if you don't have one just put them into a plastic food bag and crush with a rolling pin.

1/2 cup margarine
8 oz. chocolate graham crackers or striped
    shortbread cookies, finely crushed
3 (8-oz.) packages full-fat cream cheese,
    softened
3/4 cup superfine sugar
5 eggs

1 large lemon, finely grated zest and juice
3 oz. white chocolate, melted
1/2 cup brown sugar
4 tbsp. maple syrup
2 tsp. milk
2 tbsp. unsalted butter
1/2 tsp. vanilla extract
1 cup pecan halves

Preheat the oven to 375°F (190°C). Grease the base of a 9-in. (23-cm.) tart pan with a removable base. Melt the margarine in a double boiler. Stir in the crushed graham crackers and mix until well combined. Press the crumb mixture into the base of the pan and smooth with the back of a spoon. Beat the cream cheese in a medium bowl until smooth. Add the superfine sugar, 4 eggs, lemon zest and juice, and chocolate and beat with an electric mixer until the mixture is smooth and creamy. Spoon over the crumb crust. Bake for 15 minutes. Place the brown sugar, maple syrup, milk, butter, and vanilla in a saucepan and heat gently until melted. Chop 3/4 cup of the pecans and beat the remaining egg in a small bowl. Add both to the syrup mixture and stir well. Gently pour this mixture over the cheesecake and cook for 15 minutes more, or until firm to the touch. Set the pan on a wire rack to cool. Transfer to the refrigerator and chill for 2 hours before serving. Decorate with the remaining pecan halves and serve with Greek yogurt if desired.

Serves 8

white & semisweet chocolate cheesecake

see variations page 217

This stunning dessert is a recipe that is sure to be turned to time and time again.

8 oz. chocolate graham crackers
2/3 cup unsalted butter
12 oz. white chocolate
1 cup whipping cream
2 1/2 8-oz. packages full-fat cream cheese,
    softened

5 tbsp. superfine sugar
1 1/2 tbsp. all-purpose flour
1 tsp. vanilla extract
3 eggs
4 oz. semisweet chocolate

Preheat the oven to 350°F (175°C). Put the graham crackers in a food processor and process until crushed. Melt 1/2 cup of the butter in a saucepan and pour into the cracker crumbs. Process until combined. Spoon the mixture into an 8-in. (20-cm.) tart pan with a removable base. Using the back of a spoon push the mixture over the base and sides. Freeze for 30 minutes. Put 1/2 of the white chocolate and 2/3 of the cream in a double boiler and heat until melted. Beat the cream cheese, sugar, flour, and vanilla in a bowl until smooth. Beat in the eggs, one at a time, then add the melted chocolate until the mixture is soft and creamy. Pour into the crumb crust, level the top with a spoon, and bake for 45 minutes. Cover with aluminum foil and bake for 15 minutes more. Remove from the oven and cool in the pan. Then chill in the refrigerator for 2 hours. Melt the remaining white chocolate in a double boiler, then spread on a parchment paper-lined cookie sheet to harden. Place the remaining

butter, cream, and semisweet chocolate in a nonstick saucepan and heat gently until melted. Stir until smooth then pour over the chilled cheesecake. Chill in the refrigerator for 1 hour. To make the chocolate shavings draw the blade of a long sharp knife at an angle across the set white chocolate. Use to decorate. The cheesecake can be made up to 1 day in advance.

Serves 8

mandarin & chocolate cheesecake

see variations page 218

Kids will love this fluffy mousselike cheesecake with white chocolate and mandarins.

8 oz. chocolate graham crackers
1/2 cup unsalted butter
1 1/2 8-oz. packages low-fat cream
    cheese, softened
1 lemon, zest and juice
2/3 cup sour cream

3 eggs, separated
1/4 cup superfine sugar
1 tbsp. gelatin
2 (14-oz.) cans mandarin segments
    in natural juice
1/3 cup white chocolate chips

Put the graham crackers in a food processor and process until crushed. Melt the butter in a saucepan and add to the graham cracker crumbs while processing. Grease an 8-in. (20-cm.) tart pan with a removable base. Turn the mixture into the pan and line the base and sides, pressing the mixture down with the back of a spoon. Chill for 30 minutes in the refrigerator. Put the cream cheese, lemon zest, 3 tablespoons of lemon juice, and sour cream in a food processor and blend until smooth. In a medium bowl, beat the egg yolks and sugar until smooth and creamy. Dissolve the gelatin in 3 tablespoons water in a double boiler. Allow to cool for 5 minutes. Add the creamed egg and gelatin to the cream cheese mixture and process until smooth. In a medium bowl, beat the egg whites with an electric mixer until stiff peaks form. Drain 1 can of mandarins and reserve the juice. Roughly chop the segments and stir into the cream cheese mixture. Fold in the egg whites and chocolate chips and stir gently to combine.

Spoon the mixture into the prepared pan and chill in the refrigerator until set. Put the marmalade and reserved fruit juice into a saucepan and simmer until the mixture thickens. Remove the cheesecake from the refrigerator, and transfer to a dinner plate. Drain the remaining mandarin segments and use to decorate the cheesecake. Drizzle with the marmalade glaze and chill in the refrigerator until required. Store refrigerated for up to 2 days.

Serves 8-10

strawberry & chocolate marshmallow bars

see variations page 219

A little bit like a cheesecake, a little bit like a mousse, these fluffy and light bars make a great birthday party dessert for children too old for a novelty party cake.

8 oz. package chocolate graham crackers
    or striped shortbread cookies, crushed
1/2 cup unsalted butter, melted
1/2 cup dry flaked coconut
8-oz. package low-fat cream cheese
1 1/4 cups whipping cream
2 1/4 cups pink marshmallows

1/3 cup white chocolate chips
1 1/2 cups strawberries
1 tbsp. unflavored gelatin
4 tbsp. cold water
2 1/4 cups white marshmallows
1 tbsp. milk
4 tbsp. flaked coconut, toasted

Preheat the oven to 350°F (175°C). Grease a 7 1/2 x 9-in. (19 x 23.-cm.) jelly roll pan and line the base with parchment paper. Stir the first 3 ingredients together in a bowl and spoon into the prepared pan. Smooth with the back of a wooden spoon. Chill in the refrigerator for 30 minutes. Put the cheese, cream, marshmallows, white chocolate, and strawberries in a food processor and process until smooth. Place the gelatin and water in a double boiler. When dissolved, stir into the strawberry mixture. Spoon over the chilled base and return to the refrigerator for 2 hours. Put the marshmallows and milk in a saucepan and heat very gently until melted. Allow to cool for 5 minutes. Spread over the chilled filling and sprinkle with coconut. Refrigerate until set. Store in an airtight container for up to 2 days.

Makes 12

variations

chocolate baklava

see base recipe page 195

spiced chocolate baklava
Prepare the basic recipe, stirring 1/2 teaspoon ground allspice, 1/2 teaspoon ground nutmeg, and 1/4 teaspoon ground cloves into the nut mixture.

chocolate baklava with rose water syrup
Prepare the basic recipe, stirring 1 to 2 teaspoons rosewater extract into the cooled syrup.

mixed nut chocolate baklava
Prepare the basic recipe, replacing the walnuts and pistachios with 2 cups of mixed nuts of your choice.

white chocolate baklava
Prepare the basic recipe, omitting the semisweet chocolate and replacing with 1/2 cup white chocolate chips.

chocolate baklava petit fours
Prepare the basic recipe. With a sharp knife, cut the pastry into 32 squares. To serve, lift each square into a small foil petits fours case.

variations

marzipan & chocolate braid

see base recipe page 196

marzipan & chocolate ring
Prepare the basic recipe, but do not braid the dough. Put the dough on the
cookie sheet in a ring shape pinching the ends together. Using a sharp knife
slash the ring 12 times to expose the filling. Proceed with the recipe.

tropical chocolate braid
Prepare the basic recipe, replacing the apricots with 1 cup chopped, dried
mixed pineapple and mango. Replace the milk chocolate chunks with 2 oz.
orange-flavored chocolate chunks (see page 10).

sticky marzipan & chocolate braid
Prepare the basic recipe, replacing the frosting with 4 oz. melted semisweet
chocolate drizzled over the braid before sprinkling with the sliced almonds.

marzipan & white chocolate ring
Prepare the basic recipe, replacing the milk chocolate with 2 oz. white
chocolate chunks. Omit making the frosting and instead drizzle the ring
with 3 oz. melted white chocolate.

fruity marzipan & chocolate braid
Prepare the basic recipe adding 1/2 cup mixed dried cranberries and
blueberries with the apricots.

brownie tart

see base recipe page 199

polka-dot brownie tart
Prepare the basic recipe, arranging 1/4 cup white chocolate chips, pointy side down, in a pattern over the chocolate mixture once it has been spread in the tart pan.

brownie tart with walnuts
Prepare the basic recipe, stirring in 1/4 cup chopped walnuts once the flour mixture has been combined.

brownie tart with mandarin oranges
Prepare the basic recipe, arranging 1 cup drained canned mandarin slices in concentric circles over the top of the cooled tart.

brownie tart with white chocolate drizzle
Prepare the basic recipe, drizzling 1/4 cup melted white chocolate in lines over the cooled tart.

mocha brownie tart
Prepare the basic recipe, adding 1 teaspoon instant coffee granules to the chocolate mixture once removed from heat. Stir until the coffee has dissolved.

variations

pecan tart

see base recipe page 201

pecan & walnut tart
Prepare the basic recipe, replacing half the pecans with 1/2 cup walnut halves.

pecan & macadamia tart
Prepare the basic recipe, replacing half the pecans with 1/2 cup roughly chopped macadamias.

mixed nut tart
Prepare the basic recipe, replacing the pecans with 1 cup of mixed nuts of your choice.

gluten-free pecan tart
Prepare the basic recipe, replacing the flour and cocoa with an equal quantity of equivalent gluten-free products (see page 10).

pecan & pistachio tart
Prepare the basic recipe, replacing half the pecans with 1/2 cup roughly chopped pistachios.

unsweetened chocolate & raspberry tartlets

see base recipe page 202

unsweetened chocolate & black cherry tartlets
Prepare the basic recipe, replacing the rum with 2 tablespoons Kirsch and the raspberries with 1 lb. washed, pitted, black cherries.

white chocolate & strawberry tartlets
Prepare the basic recipe, replacing the rum with 1/2 teaspoon vanilla extract. Replace the unsweetened chocolate with 10 oz. white chocolate and the raspberries with 3 cups washed, sliced strawberries.

unsweetened chocolate & mango tartlets
Prepare the basic recipe, replacing the rum with 2 tablespoons white rum. Replace the raspberries with 1 large peeled, pitted, and sliced mango, and decorate with toasted flaked coconut.

milk chocolate & summer berry tartlets
Prepare the basic recipe, replacing the semisweet chocolate with 10 oz. milk chocolate. Replace the raspberries with 1 lb. mixed fresh raspberries, strawberries, and blueberries.

variations

baked maple–pecan cheesecake

see base recipe page 205

mixed nut fudge cheesecake
Omit the pecans in the basic mixture and replace with 1 cup mixed nuts
such as macadamias, brazils, pecans, almonds, and hazelnuts.

coffee pecan fudge cheesecake
Omit the lemon zest and juice in the basic mixture and replace with
2 tablespoons prepared espresso, cooled.

orange pecan fudge cheesecake
Omit the lemon rind and juice in the basic mixture and replace with
the zest and juice of 1 orange.

ginger & pecan cheesecake
Prepare the basic recipe, replacing the graham crackers with
8 oz. crushed gingersnaps.

pecan & macadamia cheesecake
Prepare the basic recipe, replacing half the pecans with 1/2 cup coarsely
chopped macadamia nuts.

variations

white & semisweet chocolate cheesecake

see base recipe page 206

citrus & chocolate cheesecake
Prepare the basic recipe, omitting the vanilla extract. Add the finely grated rind of 1 lemon and 1 orange and 1/2 teaspoon orange extract to the cheesecake filling mixture.

white & semisweet chocolate ginger cheesecake
Prepare the basic recipe, omitting the vanilla extract. Add 1/4 cup finely chopped preserved ginger and 1 tablespoon of the ginger syrup from the jar to the cheesecake filling mixture.

chocolate & raspberry cheesecake
Prepare the basic recipe, omitting 6 oz. of the white chocolate. Replace the white chocolate decoration with 1 1/3 cups raspberries and fresh mint leaves and dust with confectioners' sugar.

white & chocolate cherry cheesecake
Prepare the basic recipe, arranging 2 cups pitted red cherries on top of the cookie base.

white & chocolate mango cheesecake
Prepare the basic recipe, arranging 1/2 large, sliced fresh mango on top of the cookie base.

variations

mandarin & chocolate cheesecake

see base recipe page 208

raspberry & chocolate cheesecake
Prepare the basic recipe, replacing the mandarin with two 14-oz. cans of raspberries in natural juice.

apricot & chocolate cheesecake
Prepare the basic recipe, replacing the mandarin with two 14-oz. cans of apricot halves in natural juice.

peach & chocolate cheesecake
Prepare the basic recipe, replacing the mandarin with two 14-oz. cans of sliced peaches in natural juice.

mixed berry & chocolate cheesecake
Prepare the basic recipe, replacing the mandarin with two 14-oz. cans of mixed berries in natural juice.

red cherry & chocolate cheesecake
Prepare the basic recipe, replacing the mandarin with two 14-oz. cans of red cherries in natural juice.

variations

strawberry & chocolate marshmallow bars

see base recipe page 211

strawberry & chocolate mini marshmallow cheesecakes
Prepare the basic recipe, using a cookie cutter to cut out round mini cheesecakes or layer the crust and filling into individual round pans.

raspberry & chocolate marshmallow bars
Prepare the basic recipe, replacing the strawberries with
1 1/2 cups raspberries.

blackberry & chocolate marshmallow bars
Prepare the basic recipe, replacing the strawberries with
1 1/3 cups blackberries.

cherry & chocolate marshmallow bars
Prepare the basic recipe, replacing the strawberries with 2 cups pitted and halved red or black cherries.

banana & chocolate marshmallow bars
Prepare the basic recipe, replacing the strawberries with 2 cups sliced bananas tossed in 1 tablespoon lemon juice.

mousses &
ice creams

This chapter is packed with a mouthwatering
selection of creamy mousses, velvety ice creams, and
stunning ice cream bombes. Loved by everyone, these
versatile treats make great desserts for all.

ginger, saffron & chocolate slice

see variations page 233

Saffron gives this wonderful ice cream its beautiful yellow color and sophisticated flavor.

2 1/2 cups whole milk
1/4 cup preserved ginger, finely chopped
1 tbsp. ginger syrup from the jar
   of preserved ginger
5 tbsp. honey
1 1/2 tsp. ground ginger

small pinch of saffron threads
6 egg yolks
3/4 cup plus 2 tbsp. whipping cream
1 quantity of chocolate hazelnut ice cream
   (page 221)
12 chocolate leaves to decorate

Put the milk, ginger, syrup, honey, ground ginger, and saffron in a saucepan and bring to a boil. Immediately remove from heat and set aside for 30 minutes to infuse. Beat the egg yolks in a large bowl with an electric mixer. Stir in the infused milk. Pour into a clean saucepan and stir continuously over a low heat until the mixture coats the back of a spoon. Cool and chill in the refrigerator for 3 hours. Place an empty 2-lb. (1-l.) loaf pan in the freezer. Beat the cream using an electric mixer until soft peaks form. Fold into the chilled mixture. Pour into an electric ice cream maker and churn until stiff. Transfer into an airtight plastic container, cover, and freeze until solid. Spread 1/4 of the chocolate ice cream in the base of the chilled loaf pan. Freeze until solid. Spread 2/3 of the remaining ice cream up the sides of the loaf pan. Freeze until solid. Fill the center with the ginger ice cream. Smooth flat and top with the remaining chocolate ice cream. Smooth, cover with plastic wrap, and freeze until solid. Invert onto a dinner plate, decorate with chocolate leaves, and serve immediately.

Serves 8-10

classic mint chocolate chip ice cream

see variations page 234

Although traditional mint chocolate chip ice cream is always green and very minty, this sophisticated recipe has a more adult flavor.

2 1/2 cups whole milk
1 cup superfine sugar
1 oz. light corn syrup
1 1/4 cups heavy cream
4 egg yolks

2 oz. mint-flavored semisweet chocolate,
    roughly grated (see page 10)
mint extract (optional)
green food coloring (optional)

Put the milk, 1/2 the sugar, glucose, and cream in a saucepan and heat gently until almost at a boil. In a medium bowl, beat together the remaining sugar and egg yolks until pale and creamy. Beat in the hot milk mixture.

Return to the saucepan and heat gently until it thickens and coats the back of a wooden spoon, do not boil. Chill in the refrigerator for 3 hours.

Stir in the grated chocolate. Taste the mixture and add as much mint extract and food color as required. Pour the mixture into an ice cream maker and churn until thick. Spoon into an airtight plastic container. Freeze until required.

Serves 4

kahlua coffee bombe with bitter mocha sauce

see variations page 235

The bitterness of the coffee combined with the sweetness of the chocolate and meringue, makes this bombe truly mouthwatering.

3 large eggs, separated
2/3 cup superfine sugar
5 tbsp. Kahlua
2 cups whipping cream
5 oz. store-bought meringues, crushed
1 tbsp. prepared espresso coffee, cold

1 1/4 cups whipping cream
3 oz. semisweet chocolate
1 tsp. unsalted butter
7 amaretti, crushed
2/3 cup whipping cream
12 chocolate-coated coffee beans

In a medium bowl beat the egg yolks and sugar with a wooden spoon until thick and smooth. Stir in the Kahlua until well combined. In a separate bowl, whisk 2 cups cream with an electric mixer until soft peaks form. Fold in the crushed meringue and the creamed egg and sugar mixture. Beat the egg whites with an electric mixer until stiff peaks form. Lightly fold the egg whites into the Kahlua mixture. Spoon into a 3-pt. (1.5-l.) bowl or bombe mold and freeze until firm. One hour before serving remove from the freezer and place in the refrigerator for an hour. Put the coffee and 1 1/4 cups cream in a saucepan and heat until almost at a boil. Set aside for 30 minutes. Melt the chocolate in a double boiler. Remove

from the heat. Strain the infused coffee cream through a sieve into the melted chocolate. Add the butter and stir until smooth. Invert the bombe onto a dinner plate and pat the amaretti crumbs over the top and sides. Beat the remaining cream with an electric mixer until soft peaks form, and pipe swirls around the top of the bombe. Decorate with chocolate-coated coffee beans and serve with the warm sauce.

Serves 6-8

double chocolate mousse

see variations page 236

This is a very rich mousse. As the quantities are generous, you can also divide the mixture into 8 and serve in smaller glasses or espresso cups.

6 oz. white chocolate
1 tbsp. Cointreau liqueur
2 1/2 tbsp. water
1 1/4 cups whipping cream

4 oz. mint-flavored semisweet chocolate
   (see page 10)
2 eggs, separated
fresh mint leaves, to decorate
decorative chocolate leaves, to decorate

Chill 4 large wine glasses. Put the white chocolate, liqueur, and water in a double boiler and heat. Beat the cream with an electric mixer until soft peaks form. Fold into the melted white chocolate. Divide the mixture between the glasses and set in the refrigerator at an angle. Chill for 2 hours.

Melt the mint chocolate in a double boiler. Stir in the egg yolks. Beat the egg whites in a medium bowl with an electric mixer, until stiff peaks form. Fold into the melted chocolate. Pour the mint chocolate on top of the white mousse and chill for 3 to 4 hours.

Decorate with chocolate leaves and fresh mint leaves and serve.

Serves 4

triple chocolate terrine

see variations page 237

Keep this on standby in the freezer and you'll never be stuck for dessert again. But beware! It is very rich, so slice thinly and let guests come back for seconds if they dare!

10 oz. white chocolate, broken into pieces
10 oz. semisweet chocolate, broken
   into pieces

10 oz. milk chocolate, broken into pieces
3 3/4 cups whipping cream

Place the 3 chocolates in 3 separate saucepans. Put 1/3 of the cream into each saucepan and heat gently. Remove the saucepans from the heat, stir until smooth, and set aside to cool completely.

Line a 2-pt. (1-l.) loaf pan with plastic wrap. Transfer the white chocolate mixture to a bowl and beat with an electric mixer until light and fluffy. Spoon into the prepared pan and level with the back of a spoon. Freeze for 15 minutes. Beat the milk chocolate in the same way and spread the mousse over the white chocolate layer. Return to the freezer. Repeat with the semisweet chocolate and layer the mousse as before. Cover the terrine with plastic wrap and freeze overnight.

Remove from the freezer 15 minutes before serving. Invert onto a serving plate, remove the plastic wrap, and serve immediately. Run a knife under hot water before slicing.

Serves 10-12

little pots of chocolate

see variations page 238

Devilishly wicked and definitely not for those poor souls on diets!

1 1/4 cups whipping cream
6 oz. semisweet chocolate, broken into pieces
2 eggs

2 tbsp. cold strong black coffee
2 tbsp. Kahlua

Put the cream in a saucepan and heat until almost at a boil, then set aside.

Put the remaining ingredients in a food processor, and process to combine. Pour the hot cream through the lid and continue processing until evenly colored.

Divide the mixture between 6 espresso cups and chill in the refrigerator for 2 hours.

Store in the refrigerator for up to 3 days.

Serves 6

rich chocolate & hazelnut ice cream

see variations page 239

The combination of silky chocolate ice cream and crunchy toasted hazelnuts is wonderful. This recipe is suitable for making by hand or using an ice cream maker.

2 1/2 cups whole milk
2 vanilla beans, split lengthways or
     1/4 tsp. vanilla extract
6 large egg yolks

3/4 cup superfine sugar
12 oz. semisweet chocolate, broken into pieces
1 1/4 cups whipping cream
1/2 cup chopped toasted hazelnuts

Put the milk and vanilla beans in a saucepan and bring the milk almost to a boil. Remove from the heat and allow to infuse for 30 minutes before removing the vanilla beans. Combine the egg yolks and sugar in a large bowl. Beat with an electric mixer until pale and smooth. Gradually stir in the vanilla milk, then pour into a clean saucepan. Stir the vanilla mixture continuously over a very low heat until it begins to thicken and coat the back of the spoon. Do not boil. Remove from the heat.

Melt the chocolate in a double boiler. Spoon into the vanilla mixture and stir until smooth. Cover with a sheet of dampened parchment paper and chill for 1 hour. Beat the cream with an electric mixer until soft peaks form. Fold into the chocolate mixture along with the hazelnuts. Pour into the ice cream machine and churn until thick. Spoon into a plastic container, cover, and freeze until solid. Store in the freezer until required.

Serves 6

variations

ginger, saffron & chocolate slice

see base recipe page 221

layered ginger, saffron & chocolate slice
Prepare the basic recipe. Spoon the ice creams alternately into the loaf pan in 4 layers, sprinkling each layer with 1 tablespoon crushed praline (use recipe page 168).

ginger, saffron & chocolate bombe
Make the dessert in a 2-pt. (1-l.) bowl lined with plastic wrap. When solid, turn out onto a dinner plate and cover with 6 tablespoons grated semisweet chocolate. Pipe whipped cream around the base and decorate with sliced preserved ginger. Serve immediately.

ginger marmalade & saffron & chocolate slice
Prepare the basic recipe replacing the honey with 5 tablespoons of ginger marmalade.

vanilla & chocolate slice
Prepare the basic recipe omitting the preserved ginger, ginger syrup, ground ginger, and saffron and replacing with a vanilla bean split lengthways.

variations

classic mint chocolate chip ice cream

see base recipe page 223

skinny mint chocolate chip ice cream
Prepare the basic recipe, replacing the whole milk with skim milk and
replacing the whipping cream with a low-fat alternative.

white mint chocolate chip ice cream
Prepare the basic recipe, adding 2 oz. white chocolate, roughly grated.

mint chocolate chip & shortbread ice cream
Prepare the basic recipe. Crumble 1/2 cup of shortbread. Spoon
tablespoonfuls of the churned ice cream into a plastic food container,
sprinkle each with a little crumbled shortbread and give each a small dollop
of store-bought chocolate dessert sauce. Freeze until solid.

mint crisp chocolate chip ice cream
Prepare the basic recipe. Put 8 mint-flavored hard candies in a plastic food
bag and crush with a rolling pin. Stir into the ice cream with the chocolate.

variations

kahlua coffee bombe with bitter mocha sauce

see base recipe page 224

chocolate bombe with bitter mocha sauce
Prepare the basic recipe, omitting the cold coffee and replacing with 2 oz.
semisweet chocolate, melted, and stirring 3/4 cup white chocolate chunks
into the bombe mixture.

praline and coffee bombe with bitter mocha sauce
Prepare the basic recipe stirring 4 tablespoons crushed praline (use the
recipe on page 168) into the bombe mixture.

coffee bombe with bitter mocha sauce
Prepare the basic recipe omitting the Kahlua and replacing with
5 tablespoons cold strong black coffee.

individual coffee cups with bitter mocha sauce
Prepare the basic recipe dividing the mixture between 6 to 8 medium coffee
cups or glasses. Level the surface and freeze. Pipe a rosette of whipped
cream into each cup and sprinkle with amaretti crumbs. Just before serving
drizzle a little sauce over each.

variations

double chocolate mousse

see base recipe page 226

zesty double chocolate mousse
Prepare the basic recipe stirring 2 teaspoons finely grated orange
zest into the mixture.

drambuie double chocolate mousse
Prepare the basic recipe replacing the Cointreau with 1 tablespoon
Drambuie.

whiskey double chocolate mousse
Prepare the basic recipe replacing the Cointreau with 1 tablespoon whiskey.

party mousse shots
Prepare the basic recipe layering the two mousses into small
shot glasses. Arrange on a tray and serve each with a teaspoon.

variations

triple chocolate terrine

see base recipe page 228

chunky chocolate terrine
Prepare the basic recipe, adding 2 oz. each of grated white-, milk-,
and semisweet chocolate to the appropriate colored mousse just
before whipping.

3-flavor chocolate terrine
Prepare the basic recipe, replacing the milk-, white-, and semisweet
chocolate with 10 oz. each of orange-flavored semisweet chocolate, mint-
flavored semisweet chocolate (see page 10), and 70% cocoa chocolate.

chocolate praline terrine
Prepare the basic recipe, stirring 1/4 cup praline (use the recipe on page 168)
into each of the chocolate mousses just before whipping.

party chocolate terrine bites
Prepare the basic recipe, layering the mixture into ice cube trays instead of
a loaf pan. The number made depends on the size of the molds. Freeze until
solid. Turn into an ice bowl and serve with cocktail sticks so that guests can
help themselves.

variations

little pots of chocolate

see base recipe page 231

little pots of praline chocolate
Prepare the basic recipe, substituting milk chocolate for semisweet chocolate and stirring in 3 tablespoons of coarsely crushed praline (use the recipe on page 168).

little pots of orange chocolate
Prepare the basic recipe, replacing the semisweet chocolate with orange-flavored semisweet chocolate (see page 10). Replace the coffee and Kahlua with 2 tablespoons Cointreau, 2 tablespoons orange juice, and 1 tablespoon finely grated orange zest.

little pots of white chocolate
Prepare the basic recipe, replacing the semisweet chocolate with white nougat chocolate. Replace the coffee and Kahlua with 1 tablespoon honey and 3 tablespoons milk.

baileys chocolate pots
Prepare the basic recipe, omitting the semisweet chocolate, cold coffee, and Kahlua and replacing with 6 oz. milk chocolate and 4 tablespoons Baileys liqueur.

rich chocolate & hazelnut ice cream

see base recipe page 232

rich chocolate & almond ice cream
Prepare the basic recipe replacing the hazelnuts and with 1 cup chopped toasted almonds.

rich chocolate & hazelnut swirl ice cream
Prepare the basic recipe. Spoon tablespoons of the churned ice cream into a plastic container and give each a small dollop of store-bought chocolate dessert sauce. Freeze until solid.

rich chocolate & cherry ice cream
Prepare the basic recipe replacing the hazelnuts with 1 cup roughly chopped maraschino cherries.

chocolate & hazelnut popsicles
Prepare the basic recipe. Pour the mixture into popsicle molds (the number made depends on the size of the molds). Add wooden popsicle sticks and freeze until solid.

petits fours & candies

Whether you give these treats as a
gift, make them for a dinner party, or
sell them at a Christmas fair, you'll
always wish you had made more!

mini fruit chocolate bars

see variations page 253

An ice-cube tray is perfect for making these miniature bars of chocolate.

6 oz. milk chocolate
2 tbsp. chopped sweetened dried cranberries

2 tbsp. chopped orange candied peel

Melt the chocolate in a double boiler.

Wash and dry an ice-cube tray. Distribute the chocolate between the compartments of the tray, ensuring that the chocolate is approximately 1/2-in. (1-cm.) deep.

Scatter the chopped cranberries and candied peel over the chocolate, pressing them in slightly so that they sink into the chocolate.

Chill in the refrigerator until set.

Makes 7 oz. (200 g.) candies

marbled easter egg

see variations page 254

Polishing the mold first gives the finished egg a beautiful shiny sheen.

3 oz. semisweet chocolate
large Easter egg mold, approx 5 1/2-in.
   (14-cm.) long

3 oz. white chocolate
3 oz. milk chocolate

Wipe the inside of the Easter egg mold with a paper towel. Melt the semisweet chocolate in a double boiler. Remove the melted chocolate from the heat. Spoon the chocolate into a small frosting bag fitted with a small plain nozzle. Pipe swirls of chocolate inside each half of the mold, bringing the chocolate right up to the edges. Chill for 10 minutes in the refrigerator. Melt the white chocolate and repeat, piping the chocolate over the bare areas of the mold. Chill for 10 minutes. Melt the milk chocolate in the double boiler. Using a teaspoon spread the chocolate all over the inside of each half ensuring all areas of the mold are completely covered. If some areas look a little thin, melt a little more milk chocolate and recoat. Chill in the refrigerator until set. Run the tip of a sharp, unserrated knife around the top edge of each mold to remove any chocolate that may be on the flat part of the mold. Flex the mold, very gently to ease out the chocolate egg but do not remove. Melt a little extra semisweet chocolate in a double boiler. Gently remove the egg from the mold. Lightly brush the melted chocolate around the rims of the egg halves and seal together. Allow to set before wrapping in cellophane and tying with a ribbon bow.

Makes 1

chocolate–peanut butter tartlets

see variations page 255

With peanut butter, chocolate pastry, and smooth ganache, this dessert is not just for kids!

1 cup all-purpose flour
1/8 tsp. salt
1/4 cup superfine sugar
1/2 cup unsalted butter, cubed
1 egg yolk
1-2 tbsp. ice-cold water
2 tbsp. Dutch-process cocoa powder
1/2 cup smooth peanut butter

1/2 cup cream cheese, softened
2 tbsp. unsalted butter, softened
1/4 cup granulated sugar
1/2 tsp. vanilla extract
1/2 cup whipping cream
4 oz. unsweetened chocolate, finely chopped
1/2 cup whipping cream
1/4 cup peanut halves

Combine flour, salt, and superfine sugar in a medium bowl. Cut in the cubed butter to the flour mixture until it resembles damp sand. Using a fork beat the egg with the cold water. Pour the egg mixture over the flour, stirring only until the mixture has become moistened. The dough should hold the form of a ball. Cover the ball with plastic wrap and chill in the refrigerator for 30 minutes. Preheat the oven to 425°F (220°C). Place a cookie sheet in the oven. On a lightly floured surface, roll out the crust. Using a 5-in. (13-cm.) round cutter, cut out circles of pastry. Gently press the circles into 4-in. (10-cm.) individual tartlet pans with removable bottoms. Trim the excess from the edges, collect the scraps, roll out, and repeat. One crust recipe should yield 8 shells. Place the tartlet pans on the hot cookie sheet. Bake blind for 5 minutes. Take out of the oven and remove the paper and weights. Lower the temperature to 350°F (175°C) and bake for up to 5 minutes more, until the crust has darkened. Transfer to a wire rack to cool. Cream the peanut butter, cream cheese, and butter using an electric mixer on high speed. Slowly add the sugar

Makes 8

and beat until fluffy. Stir in the vanilla. In another bowl, beat the cream until soft peaks form. Fold the cream into the peanut butter mixture. Fill the tart shells 2/3 full with the filling. Cover with plastic wrap and chill for 2 hours. Heat the whipping cream in a small, heavy saucepan to boiling. Pour the hot cream over the chocolate in a heatproof bowl. Stir until the chocolate has melted and the ganache is smooth. Cool for 30 minutes. Spread over the tops of the tartlets and refrigerate for 2 hours, until the ganache is solid. Garnish each tartlet with one peanut half.

rich chocolate truffles

see variations page 256

These truffles are delicious served with coffee at the end of a meal or can be boxed, wrapped, and given as a delightful gift.

3 oz. semisweet chocolate
3 oz. milk chocolate
1/4 cup unsalted butter
1/2 cup whipping cream

3 tbsp. light or dark rum
1/3 cup ground almonds
Dutch-process cocoa powder, for coating

Melt the semisweet chocolate and milk chocolate in a double boiler. Remove from the heat and stir in the butter, stirring until smooth. Stir in the cream, rum, and almonds and chill for 2 hours until firm.

Roll teaspoon-size portions into balls, place on a cookie sheet or dinner plate, and chill for 1 hour in the refrigerator.

Roll each truffle in cocoa and place in a petit four case.

Store in an airtight container in the refrigerator until required.

Makes 24-30

spiked christmas log truffles

see variations page 257

A miniature version of the classic Christmas log and an ideal accompaniment to a cup of hot chocolate.

3/4 cup plus 2 tbsp. whipping cream
1 lb. semisweet chocolate, broken into pieces
1/2 cup brandy
1/2 cup chopped roasted hazelnuts

1/4 cup Dutch-process cocoa powder
2 oz. ready-to-roll fondant frosting
green and red food coloring
small holly leaf cutter

Put the cream in a saucepan and bring to a boil. Remove from the heat, add the chocolate, and stir until smooth and creamy. Allow to cool for 15 minutes. Stir in the brandy, then divide the mixture between 2 bowls. Stir the nuts into 1 bowl and stir well. Cover both bowls with plastic wrap and chill in the refrigerator for 3 hours. Spoon the nutty mixture into a frosting bag fitted with a large plain nozzle. Pipe long strips onto a cookie sheet lined with parchment paper. Score along the length of each with a fork to resemble tree bark. Transfer to the refrigerator to set. Divide the second bowl of chilled cream and chocolate into 15 portions and roll into small even-sized truffle balls and dust with cocoa. Using a sharp knife, cut the piped nutty chocolate strips into twenty 1-in. (2.5-cm.) pieces. Dust the logs with cocoa. Put each truffle into a petits-fours cup and decorate. Color 3/4 of the fondant frosting green and the remainder red. Roll out the green fondant thinly on a surface dusted

with confectioners' sugar and using a small holly-leaf cookie cutter, cut 35 leaves. Roll the red fondant into holly berries and press a holly leaf and berry into the top of each truffle. Store refrigerated in a sealed container for up to 7 days.

Makes 35

spiked chocolate cups

see variations page 258

Serve these petits fours with cups of steaming hot chocolate. Add one to each drink and as the chocolate melts, the drink is infused with a surprise spiked twist.

6 oz. chocolate of your choice   1/2 cup liqueur or spirit of your choice

Melt the chocolate in a double boiler.

Using 2/3 of the chocolate, thickly coat the base and sides of 20 small petits-fours paper cups using the back of a teaspoon. Place the cups, inverted, on a wire rack to set.

Using a petits-fours paper cup as a guide, draw 20 circles onto a sheet of parchment paper. Place a dollop of the remaining melted chocolate in the middle of each circle and spread out with the back of a teaspoon. Transfer the chocolate disc-covered parchment paper to a wire rack to set.

Fill the chocolate cups 2/3 full with liqueur. Using a palate knife gently ease the cooled chocolate discs from the parchment paper and set aside. Melt the extra chocolate in a double boiler. To affix the lids, brush a little melted chocolate around the edge of each chocolate disc, lift into place, and press down very gently.

Transfer to a wire rack to set completely.

Makes 20

chocolate almond clusters

see variations page 259

These irresistible treats will disappear before your eyes. Make more than you need because one portion is never enough.

1 cup whole blanched almonds
3 oz. fine semisweet chocolate

Dutch-process cocoa powder, for coating

Preheat the oven to 400°F (200°C). Put the almonds in a roasting pan and bake for 5 minutes or until golden.

Melt the chocolate in a double boiler. Add the warm almonds to the chocolate and stir well to coat evenly.

Dust a parchment paper-lined cookie sheet with cocoa. Spoon 30 teaspoonfuls of the mixture (with approximately 5 to 6 nuts in each spoonful) onto the cocoa-covered parchment paper.

Leave until almost completely set before rolling in the cocoa. Serve in petits-fours paper cups.

Makes approx. 30

variations

mini fruit chocolate bars

see base recipe page 241

mini pecan & blueberry chocolate bars
Prepare the basic recipe, replacing the cranberries and peel with
2 tablespoons each of chopped dried blueberries and chopped pecans.

mini caramel & nut chocolate bars
Prepare the basic recipe, replacing the milk chocolate with caramel-flavored
milk chocolate (see page 10) and the cranberries and peel with 2 tablespoons
each of chopped Brazil nuts and cashews.

marbled almond chocolate bars
Prepare the basic recipe, using 3 oz. each of semisweet and white chocolate.
Put a little of each chocolate into each section of the ice cube tray swirl
together with the tip of a wooden pick. Replace the cranberries with 2
tablespoons toasted sliced almonds.

sour cherry & coconut chocolate bars
Prepare the basic recipe, replacing the cranberries and peel with
1 1/2 tablespoons chopped dried sour cherries and 1 tablespoon toasted
flaked coconut.

variations

marbled easter egg

see base recipe page 243

mint crisp easter egg
Prepare the basic recipe, using only 9 oz. of semisweet mint-flavored chocolate. Melt half the chocolate and spread half inside each section of the egg mold. Allow to set for 10 minutes. Repeat with the remaining chocolate.

hazelnut & white chocolate easter egg
Prepare the basic recipe, using only 9 oz. of white chocolate. Melt half the chocolate and spread inside each section of the egg mold. Allow to set for 10 minutes. Repeat with the remaining chocolate. While still wet, sprinkle 1 tablespoon chopped roasted hazelnuts into each section of the egg mold.

truffle easter egg
Prepare the basic recipe, using only 9 oz. of milk chocolate. Melt half the chocolate and spread inside each section of the egg mold. Allow to set for 10 minutes; repeat with the remaining chocolate. Fill one half of the egg with truffles (page 246) before sealing the halves together.

fruit & nut easter egg
Prepare the basic recipe, using only 9 oz. milk chocolate. Melt half the chocolate and spread half inside each section of the egg mold. Roughly chop 1/3 cup mixed dried fruit and nuts and scatter half inside each egg half. Allow to set.

variations

chocolate–peanut butter tartlets

see base recipe page 244

chunky peanut butter tartlets
Prepare the basic recipe, replacing the smooth peanut butter with chunky
peanut butter.

chocolate–peanut butter tartlets in sweet crust
Prepare the basic recipe, omitting the 2 tablespoons Dutch-process
cocoa powder.

chocolate–almond butter tartlets
Prepare the basic recipe, replacing the peanut butter with an equal quantity
of almond butter.

double chocolate hazelnut tartlets
Prepare the basic recipe, replacing the peanut butter with an equal quantity
of chocolate-hazelnut spread.

variations

rich chocolate truffles

see base recipe page 246

orange truffles

Prepare the basic recipe, replacing the rum with Cointreau. Chill and shape the truffles. Roll in confectioners' sugar to coat.

cherry truffles

Soak 1/2 cup washed and quartered candied cherries in 3 tablespoons brandy overnight. Make the basic mixture omitting the rum. Stir in the cherries. Chill and shape. Dip the truffles in 4 oz. white chocolate, melted, to coat completely.

rum 'n' raisin truffles

Soak 2/3 cup raisins in 4 tablespoons rum overnight. Make the basic mixture omitting the rum. Stir in the raisins. Chill and shape. Stir 2 tablespoons chopped toasted hazelnuts into 4 oz. semisweet chocolate, dip truffles in the chocolate to coat completely.

fresh vanilla truffles

Stir the seeds from 2 split vanilla beans into the basic mixture omitting the rum. Chill and shape as before. Roll in grated milk chocolate to serve.

champagne truffles

Replace the rum with 3 tablespoons Champagne or sparkling wine. Chill and shape and roll in grated white chocolate to serve.

spiked christmas log truffles

see base recipe page 248

spiked carob christmas log truffles
Prepare the basic recipe, replacing the cocoa with carob powder and the semisweet chocolate with 1 lb. orange-flavored semisweet carob.

amaretto christmas truffles
Prepare the basic recipe, replacing the brandy with 1/2 cup Amaretto liqueur. Shape the mixture into balls and roll half in cocoa and half in confectioners' sugar.

coconut rum truffles
Prepare the basic recipe, replacing the brandy with 1/2 cup Malibu liqueur or white rum. Shape all the mixture into balls and roll in 1/3 cup toasted flaked coconut.

variations

spiked chocolate cups

see base recipe page 251

chocolate cherry cups
Prepare the basic recipe, using white chocolate and Kirsch and adding
1/2 maraschino cherry to each chocolate cup.

kahlua chocolate cups
Prepare the basic recipe, using semisweet chocolate and Kahlua and adding
a chocolate-coated coffee bean to each chocolate cup.

mint chocolate cups
Prepare the basic recipe, using mint-flavored semisweet chocolate (see page
10) and crème de menthe.

orange whisky cups
Prepare the basic recipe, using orange-flavored semisweet chocolate (see
page 10) and Southern Comfort.

variations

chocolate almond clusters

see base recipe page 252

chocolate brazils
Prepare the basic recipe, replacing the almonds with 1 cup Brazil nuts.
Omit roasting the nuts, and spoon individual chocolate coated nuts onto
the paper.

chocolate peanuts & almonds
Prepare the basic recipe replacing 1/2 the almonds with unsalted peanuts
and replacing the semisweet chocolate with 3 oz. white chocolate.

white chocolate & orange macadamias
Prepare the basic recipe, replacing the almonds with 1 cup whole
macadamias and stirring 2 tablespoons shredded candied orange peel
into the chocolate.

drinks, frostings & sauces

Rich and creamy, smooth and indulgent. A chocolate dessert or cake isn't complete without a puddle of sauce, a swirl of frosting, or a silky smooth coat of glossy chocolate frosting.

chocolate buttercream frosting

see variations page 274

This fluffy frosting is perfect for decorating children's birthday cakes.

1/3 cup unsalted butter
1 1/3 cups confectioners' sugar

1/4 cup Dutch-process cocoa powder
1 tbsp. milk

In a medium bowl beat the butter until softened.

Sift the confectioners' sugar and cocoa over the butter and beat until well combined.

Add the milk to the creamed chocolate mixture and beat until soft and fluffy.

Store in an airtight container for up to 3 days.

Makes sufficient to decorate an 8-in. (20-cm.) Victoria sandwich cake

chocolate glace frosting

see variations page 275

This thin shiny frosting is perfect for drizzling on cakes, or it can be made a little thicker and used for piping.

1 1/4 cups confectioners' sugar, sifted
2 tsp. unsalted butter

1 tbsp. cocoa powder
2 tbsp. milk

Combine all the ingredients in a double boiler and heat gently.

Stir until the frosting has become smooth and glossy.

Use immediately.

Makes 1/2 cup frosting

chocolate cream cheese frosting

see variations page 276

As this frosting contains cream cheese, anything decorated with this tangy frosting
must be refrigerated.

4 oz. low-fat cream cheese   **4 oz. white chocolate, melted**
3/4 cup confectioners' sugar, sifted

Combine the ingredients in a large bowl and beat for 2 minutes until the mixture is smooth
and fluffy. If the mixture is a too thick, beat in a little milk until the mixture reaches the
desired consistency.

Spoon into an airtight container and refrigerate until required.

Makes sufficient to top an 8-in. (20-cm.) cake

milk chocolate ganache

see variations page 277

Ganache is a versatile, silky smooth, cream-based frosting that spreads and pipes. It can also be used to make truffles and fill petits fours.

1 1/4 cups whipping cream　　　　　　　　**10 oz. milk chocolate**

Combine the cream and chocolate in a saucepan and heat gently until melted. Remove from the heat and beat for 2 minutes until silky smooth. Chill until the desired consistency is reached.

Store in an airtight container in the refrigerator for up to 1 week. Before using as a frosting, bring to room temperature and beat until light and fluffy.

Makes sufficient to cover the top and sides of an 8-in. (20-cm.) round cake

milk chocolate crème patissiere

see variations page 278

This rich custard can be made with any flavor chocolate, and is the perfect filling for jelly rolls and mille feuilles.

1/2 cup superfine sugar	1 tsp. vanilla extract
3 tbsp. cornstarch	2 1/2 cups milk
4 egg yolks	2 oz. milk chocolate, finely chopped

Combine the sugar, cornstarch, egg yolks, vanilla, and 3 tablespoons milk in a bowl and stir to form a smooth paste. Pour the remaining milk into a saucepan and bring to a boil.

Remove from the heat and stir into the egg mixture.

Return the mixture to the saucepan and bring to a boil stirring continuously until thick and smooth. Remove from heat and stir in the chocolate. Stir until smooth.

Cover with dampened parchment paper, and allow to cool completely before using.

Store refrigerated in an airtight container for up to 2 days.

Makes sufficient to fill two Victoria sandwich cakes or two jelly rolls

ultimate hot chocolate

see variations page 279

A deeply indulgent drink to enjoy on a cold, dark winter night.

2 1/2 cups milk
6 oz. milk chocolate, broken into pieces
1/2 cup whipping cream

10 small marshmallows
pinch grated nutmeg
2 chocolate sticks, to serve

Combine the milk and chocolate in a saucepan and heat gently until the chocolate has melted. Stir until smooth, then heat until almost at a boil. Set aside.

Beat the cream with an electric mixer until soft peaks form.

Divide the marshmallows between 2 mugs and pour the hot chocolate milk over them.

Divide the whipped cream between the 2 mugs, add a dusting of nutmeg, and serve each each drink with a chocolate stick.

Serves 2

rich bittersweet chocolate sauce

see variations page 280

Chocolate sauce doesn't get much better than this.

8 oz. best quality bittersweet chocolate with
   70% cocoa solids
2/3 cup milk

3 tbsp. whipping cream
2 tbsp. superfine sugar
2 tbsp. unsalted butter

Melt the semisweet chocolate in a double boiler. Combine the milk, cream, and sugar in a saucepan and bring to a boil. Remove from the heat and pour onto the melted chocolate, stirring continuously.

Return the chocolate mixture to the saucepan, quickly bring to a boil, and immediately remove from the heat. Beat in the butter a little at a time until the sauce is smooth and glossy. Serve immediately.

This sauce will thicken as it cools and should be warmed in a double boiler.

Store refrigerated for up to 3 days.

Serves 6

white mint chocolate sauce

see variations page 281

This creamy sauce has a fresh flavor that goes beautifully with summer fruits and meringues.

1/2 cup milk

1 cup whipping cream

20 fresh mint leaves

9 oz. white chocolate

Place the milk and cream in a saucepan and bring to a boil. Remove from the heat, add the mint leaves, cover, and allow to infuse for 15 minutes.

Melt the white chocolate in a double boiler. Stir until smooth. Pour the infused milk mixture through a strainer into the melted chocolate. Stir until smooth. Return the sauce to the saucepan, bring to a boil, then remove from the heat, stirring continuously. Serve immediately.

This sauce will thicken as it cools and should be warmed in a double boiler.

Store refrigerated for up to 3 days.

Serves 6

variations

chocolate buttercream frosting

see base recipe page 261

light chocolate buttercream
Prepare the basic recipe, replacing the butter with an equal quantity of low-fat spread.

chocolate hazelnut buttercream frosting
Prepare the basic recipe, adding 3 tablespoons of chocolate and hazelnut spread.

chocolate orange buttercream frosting
Prepare the recipe, omitting the milk and adding 1 tablespoon finely grated orange zest and 1/2 teaspoon orange extract.

chocolate, lemon & almond buttercream frosting
Prepare the basic recipe, omitting the milk and adding 1 tablespoon finely grated lemon zest and 1/2 teaspoon almond extract.

chocolate walnut buttercream frosting
Prepare the basic recipe, adding 1/2 cup finely chopped walnuts

mocha & chocolate buttercream frosting
Prepare the basic recipe, omitting the milk and adding 1 tablespoon prepared espresso, cooled.

chocolate glace frosting

see base recipe page 263

chocolate lemon glace frosting
Prepare the basic recipe, omitting the hot milk and stirring in 1 teaspoon finely grated lemon rind and 1 to 2 tablespoons lemon juice.

chocolate orange glace frosting
Prepare the basic recipe, omitting the hot milk and stirring in 1 teaspoon finely grated orange zest and 1 to 2 tablespoons orange juice.

chocolate passion fruit glace frosting
Prepare the basic recipe, omitting the hot milk and stirring in 2 tablespoons passion fruit pulp.

chocolate coffee glace frosting
Prepare the basic recipe, omitting the hot milk and stirring in 1 teaspoon instant coffee powder granules in 1 to 2 tablespoons water.

chocolate raspberry frosting
Prepare the basic recipe, omitting the hot milk and adding 2 tablespoons crushed raspberries.

chocolate cream cheese frosting

see base recipe page 264

chocolate and mint cream cheese frosting
Prepare the basic recipe, adding 2 to 3 drops mint extract.

chocolate and orange cream cheese frosting
Prepare the basic recipe, adding 1 to 2 teaspoons finely grated orange zest.

chocolate and honey cream cheese frosting
Prepare the basic recipe, adding 1 to 2 teaspoons warmed honey.

chocolate and cherry cream cheese frosting
Prepare the basic recipe, adding 1 to teaspoons cherry preserve.

milk chocolate ganache

see base recipe page 267

semisweet chocolate ganache
Prepare the basic recipe, replacing the milk chocolate with
semisweet chocolate.

orange chocolate ganache
Prepare the basic recipe, replacing the milk chocolate with orange-flavored
semisweet chocolate (see page 10) and beat in 2 teaspoons finely grated
orange zest.

mint chocolate ganache
Prepare the basic recipe, replacing the milk chocolate with mint-flavored
chocolate (see page 10) and beat in a few drops of peppermint extract.

praline chocolate ganache
Prepare the basic recipe, beating in 3 tablespoons finely chopped praline (use
the recipe on page 168).

milk chocolate crème patissiere

see base recipe page 268

mint chocolate crème patissiere
Prepare the basic recipe, replacing the vanilla extract with peppermint extract and the milk chocolate with mint-flavored semisweet chocolate (see page 10).

citrus crème patissiere
Prepare the basic recipe, omitting the vanilla extract and stirring in 1 tablespoon each of finely grated orange and lemon zest and a few drops of orange extract.

praline crème patissiere
Prepare the basic recipe, stirring in 3 tablespoons finely chopped praline (use the recipe on page 168).

caramel & chocolate crème patissiere
Prepare the basic recipe, omitting the vanilla extract and replacing the milk chocolate with an equal quantity of caramel-flavored semisweet chocolate (see page 10).

ultimate hot chocolate

see base recipe page 270

belgian hot chocolate
Prepare the basic recipe, using only 2 cups milk. Substitute the milk chocolate with semisweet chocolate and omit all the other ingredients.

chocolate toffee hot chocolate
Prepare the basic recipe, omitting the marshmallows and chocolate sticks. Drizzle each drink with 2 teaspoons ready-made toffee sauce and sprinkle with a few pieces of finely chopped soft fudge.

mint chocolate hot chocolate
Prepare the basic recipe, substituting the milk chocolate with mint-flavored semisweet chocolate and omitting the marshmallows. Drizzle each drink with 2 teaspoons ready-made chocolate syrup and decorate with a fresh mint leaf.

ultimate dairy-free hot chocolate
Prepare the basic recipe, replacing the milk with soy milk and substituting the milk chocolate with dairy-free semisweet chocolate and omitting the cream and chocolate stick.

variations

rich bittersweet chocolate sauce

see base recipe page 271

rich milk chocolate sauce
Prepare the basic recipe, replacing the bittersweet chocolate with 8 oz. milk chocolate.

rich white chocolate sauce
Prepare the basic recipe, replacing the bittersweet chocolate with 8 oz. white chocolate.

rich mint-chocolate sauce
Prepare the basic recipe, replacing the bittersweet chocolate with 8 oz. mint-flavored semisweet chocolate (see page 10).

rich orange-chocolate sauce
Prepare the basic recipe, replacing the bittersweet chocolate with 8 oz. orange-flavored semisweet chocolate (see page 10).

white mint chocolate sauce

see base recipe page 273

light white mint chocolate sauce
Prepare the basic recipe, replacing the milk and whipping cream
with skim milk and low-fat whipping cream.

white spearmint chocolate sauce
Prepare the basic recipe, replacing the mint leaves with fresh
spearmint leaves.

milk & mint chocolate sauce
Prepare the basic recipe, replacing the white chocolate with 9 oz.
milk chocolate.

white mint & vanilla chocolate sauce
Prepare the basic recipe, replacing the mint leaves with 1 vanilla bean,
split lengthways.

index

Grandpa's Gingersnaps:

2 cups granulated sugar

1½ cups butter

2 eggs

½ cup molasses

3 ¾ flour

1 tsp. b. soda

3 tsp. ginger

2 tsp cinnamon

1 tsp. cloves - optional

½ tsp. salt

1. Preheat oven to 350 degrees
2. In medium bowl sift together flour, b. soda, cloves, ginger, cinnamon, salt
3. In another medium bowl beat together sugar, molasses and egg until well combined. Add softened butter - mix well and then add flour mixture until well combined. Refig. until chilled.
4. Roll dough into balls and then in sugar until coated. Press and place

on cookie sheet (greased).
Bake 8-10 mins and cool on rack.